Endorsements

"This invaluable work from the pen of Frank Page reflects his time-tested experience as a local church and denominational leader. Page's practical and well-written work will enable readers to think biblically and authentically about the responsibilities and challenges of leadership. *The Nehemiah Factor* brings wisdom and Spirit-directed insight to help and guide those who are called to this demanding work. I highly recommend this book."

—David S. Dockery, president
Union University

"This book is a call to wise, godly leadership firmly rooted in biblical truth. You will be encouraged and edified by the insights of Frank Page."

—Daniel L. Akin, president
Southeastern Baptist Theological Seminary

OTHER BOOKS BY FRANK PAGE

The Incredible Shrinking Church
Trouble with the TULIP
Commentary on Mark
Jonah (in *The New American Commentary* series)
The Witnessing and Giving Life

THE
NEHEMIAH
FACTOR

16 CHARACTERISTICS OF A MISSIONAL LEADER

FRANK S. PAGE, PhD

[signature: Frank S. Page]

NEW HOPE
PUBLISHERS

Birmingham, Alabama

New Hope Publishers
P. O. Box 12065
Birmingham, AL 35202-2065
www.newhopepublishers.com

New Hope Publishers is a division of WMU®

Page, Franklin S., 1952-
  The Nehemiah factor : 16 characteristics of a missional leader / by
Frank S. Page.
     p. cm.
  ISBN 978-1-59669-223-7 (sc)
  1. Bible. O.T. Nehemiah--Criticism, interpretation, etc. 2. Christian
leadership--Biblical teaching. I. Title.
  BS1365.6.L4P34 2008
  253--dc22
                              200800741

Cover design by the Design Works Group

ISBN-10: 1-59669-223-5
ISBN-13: 978-1-59669-223-7

N084146 • 0608 • 10M1

Dedication

*I dedicate this book to the churches
I have been privileged to pastor,
who have taught me many lessons
in leadership and "followship."*

Table of Contents

Introduction

In his autobiography, *Just as I Am*, Billy Graham recounts a conversation with John F. Kennedy shortly after JFK's election:

> "On the way back to the Kennedy house, the president-elect stopped the car and turned to me. 'Do you believe in the Second Coming of Jesus Christ?' he asked.
>
> 'I most certainly do.'
>
> 'Well, does *my* church believe it?'
>
> 'They have it in their creeds.'
>
> 'They don't preach it,' he said. 'They don't tell us much about it. I'd like to know what you think.'
>
> "I explained what the Bible said about Christ coming the first time, dying on the cross, rising from the dead, and then promising that He would come back again. 'Only then,' I said, 'are we going to have permanent world peace.'
>
> 'Very interesting,' he said, looking away. 'We'll have to talk more about that someday.' And he drove on."

Later the two men met again, this time at the 1963 National Prayer Breakfast.

> "I had the flu," Graham remembers. "After I gave my short talk, and he gave his, we walked out of the hotel

to his car together, as was always our custom. At the curb, he turned to me.

'Billy, could you ride back to the White House with me? I'd like to see you for a minute.'

'Mr. President, I've got a fever,' I protested. 'Not only am I weak, but I don't want to give you this thing. Couldn't we wait and talk some other time?'

It was a cold, snowy day, and I was freezing as I stood there without my overcoat.

'Of course,' he said graciously."

But the two would never meet again. Later that year, President Kennedy was assassinated. Graham writes that his hesitation at the car door still haunts him after all these years. "What was on his mind? Should I have gone with him? It was an irrecoverable moment."

Are there moments in our lives when we find ourselves at a crossroad, when the decision made in a moment can change us forever? I believe the answer is yes. There are truly pivotal times in our lives. And there are decisions made during those times that forever alter our destiny, as well as the destiny of others. These pivotal times come not only for individuals; they also come for churches, denominations, and even entire movements.

I believe this country's larger Christian community currently stands at such a moment. I know that God has been immensely blessing us. He has blessed us for a reason. It is not to make us spiritually fat and self-centered. Rather, it is to be an awesome body of believers doing His work in the world. As big a body as we are and as strong as we have become, however, we will fail in God's call if we do not experience His hand of blessing in the future. I believe we could lose that blessing and that we are at an irrecoverable moment. Is it already too late? Many now question the future of the evangelical movement because millions of Christians do not participate or have decided to no longer participate in the growth of the kingdom.

God is calling

Many factors may well spell the end of a bright future for evangelical churches. I believe God is trying to get our attention. He is calling for Christian leaders and laypeople to wake up to the realities of the twenty-first century. He is calling the body of Christ to supply missional leaders able to take advantage of the manifest opportunities before us for the glory of God.

Some believe we are moving quickly toward a European style of postmodern lethargy, where people are apathetic to and unconcerned for the church. Some say the time of the church has passed. Personally, I do not feel it is too late for our churches to grasp the opportunities God has for us. I have traveled all over this nation, and I can tell you I am cautiously optimistic about our future. I say *cautiously* because of the divisions rife among us, and the forces in our society that mitigate against the spiritual. But I am optimistic as well, and I base this not only on what I see among the people of God, but also in what I believe Scripture teaches.

Look at Ezekiel's dramatic vision for Israel's restoration as a community and a people of God:

> *The hand of the LORD was on me, and He brought me out by His Spirit and set me down in the middle of the valley; it was full of bones. He led me all around them. There were a great many of them on the surface of the valley, and they were very dry. Then He said to me, "Son of man, can these bones live?"*
>
> *I replied, "Lord GOD, [only] You know."*
>
> *He said to me, "Prophesy concerning these bones and*

say to them: Dry bones, hear the word of the LORD! This is what the Lord GOD says to these bones: I will cause breath to enter you, and you will live. I will put tendons on you, make flesh grow on you, and cover you with skin. I will put breath in you so that you come to life. Then you will know that I am the LORD."

So I prophesied as I had been commanded. While I was prophesying, there was a noise, a rattling sound, and the bones came together, bone to bone. As I looked, tendons appeared on them, flesh grew, and skin covered them, but there was no breath in them. He said to me, "Prophesy to the breath, prophesy, son of man. Say to it: This is what the Lord GOD says: Breath, come from the four winds and breathe into these slain so that they may live!" So I prophesied as He commanded me; the breath entered them, and they came to life and stood on their feet, a vast army.

Then He said to me, "Son of man, these bones are the whole house of Israel. Look how they say: Our bones are dried up, and our hope has perished; we are cut off. Therefore, prophesy and say to them: This is what the Lord GOD says: I am going to open your graves and bring you up from them, My people, and lead you into the land of Israel. You will know that I am the LORD, My people, when I open your graves and bring you up from them. I will put My Spirit in you, and you will live, and I will settle you in your own land. Then you will know that I am the LORD. I have spoken, and I will do [it]." [This is] the declaration of the LORD.

—Nehemiah 37:1–14

This is a powerful passage about a seemingly bleak situation. The passage depicts utter and complete desolation. No activity is visible anywhere on the landscape, and life is so far removed from the scene that the wind has blown away even the smell of death. Broken spears, chariots without wheels, rusty swords, and many dry, lifeless bones litter the battlefield. They are everywhere, bleached by the sun and blasted by the blowing sand. This valley once rang out with military commands, thundering at the footsteps of soldiers as they moved into position opposite each other. But now, nothing but silence. The only thing moving is a tattered regimental standard dancing in the wind on the end of a lance.

Suddenly, a man appears overlooking the valley. He too is motionless and silent, awed by a valley destitute of all living beings. Then a voice—a voice which at the same time sounds like both a thunder and a whisper—breaks the silence and asks, *"Son of man, can these bones live?"* Can springtime come when the white death of winter covers the ground?

The kingdom established by King David has been destroyed. The bones in the valley represent a nation scattered by its conquerors, the hopes of its people destroyed. If they could have returned from exile to Israel, they would have seen the desolation they felt in their hearts. This was a time of great despair and complete lack of confidence.

The question addressed to Ezekiel about Israel is both personal and national. It is a question for the fate of our nation or any nation that has lost its moral anchor. But it is also a personal question we must each ask when something dear or valuable in our personal lives dies. This is a question for every Christian leader, from the pulpit to the pew. Many have written off the church, thinking it is an archaic and bureaucratic entity that is no longer effective or relevant.

I do not agree with this. I thank God we have always had people standing strong for the church and the inerrant Word of God. The battle of inerrancy was one of extreme importance. If the church had not fought the battle, we would not even be discussing the issues we discuss today. But many of us have tunnel vision and think "the battle for the Bible" was the only important battle the evangelical church has fought. Now we must deal not just with the inerrancy of the Bible but also with its relevancy. Are we relevant in our ministries, our understanding of culture, and in our ability to relate to this world? Can these bones live? Does a chance exist for new life? Can we be effective again in our witness to the world? Can revival come?

We must be right in the battles we choose, but we must also be relevant in the lives we live. This consideration was not just for the Jewish exiles after the fall of Jerusalem. It is our question when failure, death, disappointment, or sorrow invades our lives. We all know what it means to fail, to be disloyal in things relating to our faith and our Lord, to fail to live up to the commitments we once made. How did this happen? When did God make Himself known to you for the first time? Was it in a powerful, captivating, and undeniable way? Was God that real to you? Did He burst into your life so powerfully you felt you could touch His face? Did the pure, unblemished love of God control everything you did? Did it burn in your heart, guide your thoughts, and lead you through more than one of life's storms? Was the Lord number one in your life? When did that fire start to go out? When did you come to realize something else was taking first place in your life? Has your faith experience grown cold and empty? *"Can these bones live?"* Can the dying embers of a pale and wounded faith be stirred to flame again?

He revives us again

How do you answer the voice that questioned Ezekiel? How do you respond to the hard questions of God? Before answering too easily, remember the awful struggle of Jesus in Gethsemane. Serious faith is not easy, not even for our Lord. Here is the question I want to ask and explore in this book: Can revival come through truly missional leaders of genuine faith? Can you be such a leader?

The answer is not within. But if we listen, we can hear the word of the Lord and find the answer. How do we do this when our faith is at low ebb? Can we expect to hear God speak in our loneliness and despair, even when we feel cut off from all hope? Did Ezekiel expect to hear the word of the Lord in that valley of death, that wilderness of life? Why should the Lord speak in such a place anyway? There were no ears to hear, no tongues to speak, no life to respond. Why didn't God send Ezekiel to the temple, or some other appropriate place? Why not send him to the throngs of people? Speaking the word of the Lord in that place was like a television network broadcasting its top-rated show at 3:00 A.M. Who will see it? Who will hear it?

The testimony of Scripture is that God does indeed speak His word in the valley of death and the wilderness of life, because that is exactly where the people who are most in need hear it. It's in the valley of destruction and despair where we need to know that dry bones can live again.

Jesus Christ is mighty to save, and He who conquered the grave can and does change lives. The One who lives again can give us new life today and every day. He can provide courage and perseverance to face shadows darker than the night itself. He can replenish strength even in the wilderness, and support us when we feel we just can't go on. And God certainly can raise up new leaders who are missional, leaders who can bring revival in the valley of bones and new life back to our churches.

Our dried-out bones can live again! It is the assurance of God through the prophet Ezekiel given in the valley of dry bones. And the promise of faith in Jesus Christ is the message of the entire New Testament. *"Can these bones live?"* Yes, wherever Jesus Christ is, there is glorious life and illustrious hope.

What is the Lord's response when missional leaders seek His face? Second Chronicles says, *"And [if] My people who are called by My name humble themselves, pray and seek My face, and turn from their evil ways, then I will hear from heaven, forgive their sin, and heal their land"* (7:14). Revival is what happens. God hears our prayers, forgives our sins, and heals our land. He makes dry bones live again.

CHAPTER I

A Missional Leader
Is a Person of Godly Character

Missional is the buzzword in evangelical circles today. It is so current you won't even find it in your dictionary. The word has replaced other terms, such as *missionary*, *purpose driven*, *evangelistic*, or *socially intentional*. It involves a way of looking at Christianity that integrates concern for both evangelism and social ministries. It is a kind of acting out of the faith in daily life. The word encompasses much of what Christians have simply thought of in the past as living out the Christ life.

> It is acting out faith in daily life.

There is a call for a new style of leadership that lives out the faith in a variety of settings. It is called *missional leadership*, and it offers a type of leadership providing vision and strategy for living a lifestyle that is an example for others.

Much has been written about leadership from a spiritual perspective, referring to biblical leaders, especially our Lord Jesus as our example. There are many great books available on the topic, such as *The Mark of Jesus* by George and Woodbridge,

Servant Leadership and *Lead Like Jesus* by Blanchard and Hodges, *On Track Leadership* by Kramp, and *Spiritual Leadership* by Blackaby. All of these books and hundreds of others have something important to say about being God's people in roles of leadership. I have read many of these books on leadership, and I have benefited from them. I have also been privileged to see leadership at an entirely different level. For example, I have met and spoken with several US presidential candidates and other politicians as well. The fact that I pastor a church in South Carolina, which has one of the first presidential primaries, no doubt is the reason they gave me the time of day, along with the fact that I was the president of my denomination.

During a campaign season, one hears a great deal about the leadership characteristics of candidates. We hear of character, integrity, honesty, and values. These things matter very much, and they should matter to God's people. In recent years events in the evangelical church have called all believers to a renewed understanding of character and integrity among leaders. This is especially true when it comes to sexual, ministerial, and financial ethics.

Much of what has already been published on leadership is written from a business perspective. While there are many parallels between competent leadership in the business and church worlds, higher standards should be expected in the area of church, pastoral, and other ministry leadership. It would be a wonderful thing if all Christian leaders were superintelligent and doggedly persistent, like Abraham Lincoln and Winston Churchill. It would be marvelous if all our church leaders were great strategists, such as Robert E. Lee or Dwight D. Eisenhower. Having a strong personality, like George Patton or Ronald Reagan had, would also be necessary for good and effective leadership. I suppose many of our leaders already have this last characteristic.

Missional character matters

The Old Testament Book of Nehemiah is one of the greatest case studies on leadership one can find. In a day of "live and let live," Nehemiah called God's people to account. He lived a godly example before them, and challenged them to a new and deeper commitment to the Lord. Though the biblical material about Nehemiah is relatively brief, his life is a tremendous example of devout missional leadership. The name *Nehemiah* literally means "Yahweh (God) is comfort." In both word and deed, this prophet demonstrated to his people a testimony of God's comforting goodness and power.

Nehemiah was the cupbearer to King Artaxerxes in the capital city of Susa. He had the duty of filling and handing the cups in which wine was served to the king. Nehemiah heard that his fellow Jews were not being allowed to rebuild the wall of Jerusalem, which had been broken down and its gates destroyed by fire. He recognized how dangerous the situation was for the Jews in Palestine. The changeable times, the disdain of the Samaritan leaders for the Jews of Palestine, and the almost successful extermination of the Jews by Haman were all good reasons for Nehemiah's anxiety. After prayer and with deep concern for his people in Judea, Nehemiah spoke with Artaxerxes about returning to the city of his fathers' tombs to rebuild the wall. The king agreed.

Escorted by royal soldiers and horsemen, Nehemiah arrived in Jerusalem in 445 B.C. During the period following his arrival, he saw great opposition to what he wanted to accomplish, along with great victory. It was during this period that Nehemiah exhibited the lifestyle and leadership that stands as an unusually admirable example of missional leadership.

I hope the reader is called to a time of spiritual inventory in our study of the characteristics of missional leadership. Study the passages that are referenced, and enter into a spirit of prayer.

Listen carefully to the Lord, because God wants us to hear Him and discern His heart. His desire is for all people to come to faith in His Son, and then to grow in that faith.

> *For the grace of God has appeared, with salvation for all people, instructing us to deny godlessness and worldly lusts and to live in a sensible, righteous, and godly way in the present age, while we wait for the blessed hope and the appearing of the glory of our great God and Savior, Jesus Christ. He gave Himself for us to redeem us from all lawlessness and to cleanse for Himself a special people, eager to do good works.*
> —Titus 2: 11–14

This is one of the most succinct passages in the Bible to detail the wonderful salvation God has offered to us through Jesus Christ. It is a powerful passage, showing God's desire for us in a simple yet profound way. These words can make us missional leaders.

Notice that there is a universal offering of the grace of God that has appeared to all and brings salvation to all. God's grace, then, is redemptive, not destructive. It is His unmerited favor. We agree with the concept of the total depravity of humanity, and none of us deserves any grace whatsoever. But the good news of grace is that God provided redemption for every living soul calling on His name. Titus stresses that this wonderful gift came for everyone. There is nothing difficult about understanding that salvation is available to all, as John 3:16 says. It is available to every individual, and its saving effect depends upon that

God's grace is operative to everyone.

individual's personal response of faith. God's grace is operative everywhere and to everyone, and it must be presented as such by God's missional forces all across the globe.

After close and long-term study, I have come to see very clearly that the Bible nowhere states God has elected some to salvation and others to damnation. When Scripture uses terms such as *foreordained, predestined, chosen,* and so on, it expresses biblical truths, but it is not saying anywhere that God arbitrarily chose some to be saved while others would be lost forever with no hope for salvation. He has, however, undeniably, chosen some in the church for leadership.

> **He has undeniably chosen some in the church for leadership.**

Let me state clearly that God has foreordained the *how,* not the *who.* In other words, we must recognize that He has foreordained that the way of election is accepting Jesus Christ by faith. In verses 3 to 13 of the first chapter of Ephesians, Paul uses the phrase *"in Christ"* or its equivalent 11 times.

> *Blessed be the God and Father of our Lord Jesus Christ, who has blessed us with every spiritual blessing in the heavens, in Christ."*
> *He made known to us the mystery of His will... to bring everything together in the Messiah.*
> *"In Him we were also made his inheritance.*
> —Ephesians 1:9, 10, 11

Over and over the Apostle Paul states that the way of salvation is in Christ. It is in Him that we become a part of the elect, the predestined, the foreordained body of Christ.

We must also consider the very nature of God. Is our Creator a God of loving grace, or a God of cold, calculated prejudice? Another issue of extreme importance is the issue of free will. Do we have it, or are we responsible in any way for the decisions of life? If the sovereign nature of God is such that He has preordained every aspect of salvation, which includes every part of a person's receptivity to the gospel, why are we told this?

> *"Keep asking, and it will be given to you. Keep searching, and you will find. Keep knocking, and the door will be opened to you. For everyone who asks receives, and the one who searches finds, and to the one who knocks, the door will be opened."*
> —Matthew 7:7–8

And why did Jesus tell the rich young ruler in Matthew, chapter nineteen, what was required for him to do to attain eternal life? If nothing was required because all things are already foreordained, what is the point? The rich young man went away sorrowful because he was not willing to do what Christ asked. Why didn't Jesus tell him, "It doesn't matter anyway. Either you are a part of the elect or you are not. You have no say and no responsibility in the matter." And why did Jesus weep over Jerusalem and lament that they had rejected Him? *"How often I wanted to gather your children together, as a hen gathers her chicks under her wings, yet you were not willing!"* (Matthew 23:37.) What could this mean if the people of Jerusalem could not of their own free will reject Him? No, it is clear humanity has the capacity to accept or reject the Lord.

God's plan through the ages is to redeem His creation, to provide a way for the salvation of all humanity through the blood sacrifice of His Son, Jesus. God created us to have fellowship with Him. Is it possible He would violate His own desire by offering fellowship to some but not to others? Impossible. The late Hershel Hobbs once said that "to violate man's free will would make him less than a person, only a puppet dangled on the string of fate. The Bible never teaches that. Man is free to choose but is responsible to God for his choices. Otherwise, God himself is responsible for man's sin. This is unthinkable!"

We must all accept this offer from God. It's up to us, not some predetermined cosmic conclusion. It's the greatest gift ever known, and becoming a missional leader requires personally knowing the Lord Jesus Christ. That is your choice, and mine.

God's second great wish is also accomplished by the power of His grace. Remember, His first great desire is for all people to know Christ and gain salvation. His second great desire is that all Christians grow into mature disciples while we wait for the blessed hope and the appearing of the glory of our great God. In a negative, reverse way, Satan's two greatest desires correspond to God's two great desires. He does not want us to meet Christ, and, if we do, he sure doesn't want us to grow in faith.

We are instructed to deny godlessness and worldly lusts and to live in a sensible, righteous, and godly way. This means that grace operates not only at the time of salvation, but in the daily lives of Christ's followers. Grounded in God's nature, grace makes ethical demands of us, and these demands are always consistent with the divine nature. Grace trains and instructs

> **Becoming a missional leader requires personally knowing the Lord Jesus Christ.**

believers in all things according to sound teaching. There are two parts to the process of this training, teaching, encouraging, and discipling.

The first part is negative. Grace trains us to say no to ungodliness and worldly passions. It leads believers to the place where—as a definite act of the will—we voluntarily make a double renunciation of the past. We repudiate and abandon our wicked ways, and we reject worldly desires, those cravings characteristic of a world estranged from God. The missional leader must maintain these acts of renunciation on a daily basis, becoming more holy in all spheres of our lives. This means repentance of our ungodly attitudes, ambitions, affections, and actions. We need to ask the Lord to help us become more aware of the enemy's footprints in our lives as he creeps in to destroy God's great work. Missional leaders must refuse those things contradictory to God's nature, character, and purpose for our lives.

> Missional leaders must refuse those things contradictory to God's nature, character, and purpose for our lives.

Then the second part is positive. Grace teaches us to say yes to a life that is self-controlled, serious, and upright. We are to live in the sense of coming to a life that should be consistently characterized by three qualities. Our lives must be inward or self-controlled. This is demanded of every believer. Our lives must also be outward, upright, faithfully fulfilling all the demands of truth and justice in our relations with others. And our lives must be upward, godly, and fully devoted to the supreme plan in reverence and loving obedience.

Such a life is not only possible, it is obligatory for the missional leader in this present age. Christ obeyed God our Father by giving Himself as a sacrifice for our sins and by rescuing us from this evil world (Galatians 1:4). The world holds dangers for all believers, but especially for missional leaders. We must show up every day in God's great training school if we are to grow the way God wants us to grow. In his letter to the Christians at Colossae, the Apostle Paul said,

> *Since, then, you have been raised with Christ, set your hearts on things above, where Christ is seated at the right hand of God. Set your minds on things above, not on earthly things. For you died, and your life is now hidden with Christ in God.... Put to death, therefore, whatever belongs to your earthly nature: sexual immorality, impurity, lust, evil desires and greed, which is idolatry.*
> —Colossians 3:1–3, 5 (NIV)

Character matters very much. Our character must be redeemed by the Lord as we submit to Him in faith. As we have seen in the powerful passage from the New Testament Book of Titus, our character must be developed in God's training school. As we continue taking spiritual inventories of ourselves, we should ask what grades we are getting in God's great training school. A missional leader must be a person of godly character.

Reflections

1. When you were at a crossroads in life, what decision did you make? Did this make any difference?

2. What was God's plan through the ages?

3. God has foreordained the *how*, not the *who*. What does this mean?

CHAPTER 2

A Missional Leader
Is a Person of Calling

Many people feel they are not capable of becoming leaders. Some believe one must have a specific personality type in order to be a leader of great effectiveness. While leadership admittedly is easier for some than for others, I believe great leaders can be called and developed out of any personality type.

It is true that my personality type is quite dominant. In fact, in various personality studies, I measure in the very top of the chart in the dominance section! But, as I have said, effective leaders come from different personality styles. Eric Reed and Collin Hansen wrote in the *Leadership Journal* that for most pastors there is a tension and some doubt regarding their ability to be missional leaders. They write that "many in pastoral leadership…continue to feel tension between…pastoring and leading. With high-profile CEOs and megachurch leaders as models, how do most pastors measure up? How *can* they?"

Consider the following statistics Reed and Hansen use to demonstrate this tension.

Style Guide

My leadership style is

Shepherding	55 percent
Bridge-building	53 percent
Directional	44 percent
Visionary	36 percent

My leadership style is not

Entrepreneurial	43 percent
Reengineering	38 percent
Strategizing	34 percent
Visionary	32 percent

Regardless of personality types or styles, despite doubts many have about their capacity to become missional leaders, God's calling upon any person's life comes with the potential to become a truly great missional leader. In other words, "Those whom God calls, God enables." While there are many great leaders in government, business, education, the armed forces, and in every other aspect of life, God's call upon a person's life gives that person a strength and purpose that cannot be achieved in any natural way.

> Every missional leader must have a sense of calling to the task.

No one would deny that Nehemiah had a leader's calling. It was in a powerful prayer meeting when God called Nehemiah to travel back to Israel to help the people of God by rebuilding Jerusalem's city wall. Every missional leader must have a sense of calling to the task.

God's call was experienced dramatically by Samuel, when the boy was awakened from sleep.

Samuel heard someone calling his name. Thinking it was the aged priest Eli, Samuel quickly ran to his bedside. But Eli had not called. Again, and yet again, this same thing happened. At last, Eli realized that the voice must be the voice of God. He told the boy to listen well and if the voice came again to say, *"Speak, LORD, for your servant is listening"* (1 Samuel 3:9). When the voice came the fourth time, Samuel responded to the call of the Lord and received a prophecy he was to share with God's people. In considering the call and voice of God, we should remember that it may be issued for several purposes. We know that He calls to offer salvation, and every Christian is grateful for that. In fact, Christians are often referred to as *"those who are called"* (Romans 8:28) or you *"who are Jesus Christ's by calling"* (Romans 1:6). We are also called *"saints"* (2 Corinthians 1:2), and *"those who are called according to His purpose"* (Romans 8:28). It is true that God takes the initiative in our salvation, and that through His Holy Spirit He calls us into His kingdom. God's offer of salvation is a tremendous heritage. But we are to call upon the name of the Lord to receive that salvation, and we do that by responding with our free will.

Floyd Craddock records the story of eating in a restaurant in the Great Smoky Mountains of Tennessee. He says he went there to get away from people, and was slightly bothered by an elderly man who went from table to table talking to people. Finally, the elderly man came up to him and began talking. He asked him what he did, and when Craddock replied that he was a teacher of preachers, the elderly man told him he wanted to share a preacher story.

Craddock recalls the elderly man said, when he was a little boy he lived a rough life. His mother was not married, and he was called horrid names by the other kids. He liked to go to church and would slip in late to hear the preacher deliver thundering sermons. Afterwards, he would slip out very quickly because he was afraid someone would criticize him for coming to church. One day, however, he was so caught up in the sermon that he failed to get out quick enough and consequently was caught in the rush of people leaving. When he felt a hand on his shoulder, he looked up to see the face of the preacher. The preacher looked down at him and said, "What are you doing here, boy? Wait a minute, I know who you are, I know who your daddy is. You're a child of…God's. Go claim your inheritance son."

After telling this story, the little old man toddled off to another table. Captured by his story, Craddock called out to him, "Sir, what is your name?"

The old man turned around and said, "My name is Hooper, Ben Hooper."

Then Craddock said, "I remember my daddy telling me about an illegitimate governor of the state of Tennessee named Ben Hooper."

Even though he had grown up in trying circumstances, this man became the governor of the state of Tennessee. The preacher's words challenged Craddock to see the great worth in himself and to claim his inheritance. When we see ourselves as children of God, we become aware how very important we are and that we are truly wealthy indeed.

Being a child of God is a magnificent inheritance, and God's call is always a special one. Salvation is truly the greatest of all miracles, which none of us could ever deserve or earn. Yet He gives it to us as we ask and reach out in faith.

A Great Question About Responsibility

Once, Pilate asked the greatest of all questions. Following the religious trials of Jesus, the Lord was taken to Pilate, who alone could impose the desired death sentence. Thus it was Pilate, in an auspicious moment of decision, who spelled out the critical issue that is the most pivotal matter in all of life. He asked, *"What should I do then with Jesus, who is called Messiah?"* (Matthew 27:22)

There are several ways to look at this simple but important question. Pilate knew that Jesus was not just another run-of-the-mill Jew who had offended the Jewish religious leaders. Consider what he had to ponder as he faced the question of Jesus. First there was the power of these religious leaders. Pilate resented their pressure, especially since he doubted the guilt of Jesus, but he also couldn't allow himself to be open to the charge of being lenient to one accused of treason by the religious hierarchy. He had to consider their influence. He also had to consider his own impression of Jesus, and his own impression was that Jesus was definitely innocent. Pilate was reluctant to execute Jesus because he knew a criminal revolutionary when he saw one—and Jesus was not one.

The dignified silence of the Lord made Pilate feel that it was not Jesus but he himself who was on trial. Pilate felt the power of Jesus, but was afraid to submit to it. Then he had to consider his wife's advice. That is always a wise thing for a husband to do, but this was especially important for Pilate at this particular time. The reason was that his wife had been warned in a dream to have nothing to do with Jesus, for she knew He was a righteous and just man (Matthew 27:19). No doubt she was afraid that the vengeance of heaven would follow if Pilate condemned an innocent man. Still, the advice she offered is impossible to follow because each person has do something with the Lord.

> **No decision in life is more important than one's decision about Christ.**

No decision in life is more important than one's decision about Christ. It is crucial because of who Christ is. We read in the Gospel of John that Jesus said, *"The Father and I are one"* (10:30). To claim He was one with God in purpose would have been a terrible blasphemy if not true. It is also crucial to know who Christ is because of the consequences. What one does with the question of Jesus determines life's meaning and destiny. We all need to answer for ourselves the question Pilate asked the crowd: *"What should I do then with Jesus?"* Even though Pilate asked what should be done, he acknowledged he was the one who would make the decision whether or not Jesus would be crucified. Pilate was no missional leader. One's decision about Christ determines the kind of leader one is. The missional leader in today's church understands something about spiritual inheritance, and knows that God's call to salvation is the greatest of all calls.

The choice of sin is personal, and as each person chooses to sin, therefore each must personally choose to call on Christ to be forgiven of one's sin. A member of my congregation was trying to convince a person of her need for Christ. The person rejected the gospel and said, "I know I'm going to bust hell wide open." That was her decision. One's decision about Christ is also personal because Jesus died for us as individuals. He cares for us and He would have died for any one of us alone. *"In the same way, it is not the will of your Father in heaven that one of these little ones perish"* (Matthew 18:14).

I can't stand in another person's shoes and make the decision about Christ for them, and neither can you. As Pilate made his personal decision, so each individual must do likewise. Hershel Hobbs once said, "The story goes that the devil and God held an election to decide whether each person would be saved. The devil voted against salvation. God voted for personal salvation. That made it a tie. It thus is left to each individual to cast his or her own deciding vote."

Pilate had to do something with Jesus. The decision-making encounter was thrust upon him by others, but being confronted with the issues, it was his to decide. He wanted to ignore the issue. *"So Pilate told them, 'Take Him yourselves and judge Him according to your law.' 'It's not legal for us to put to death,' the Jews declared"* (John 18:31).

Next Pilate tried to shift the decision to Herod Antipas,

> *But they kept insisting, "He stirs up the people, teaching throughout all Judea, from Galilee where He started even to here." When Pilate heard this, he asked if the man was a Galilean. Finding that He was under Herod's jurisdiction, he sent Him to Herod, who was also in Jerusalem during those days."*
> —Luke 23:5–7

Pilate even went so far as to try substituting another person for Christ.

> *"At the festival the governor's custom was to release to the crowd a prisoner they wanted. At that time they had a notorious prisoner called Barabbas. So when they had gathered together, Pilate said to them, "Who is it you want me to release for you—Barabbas, or Jesus who is called Messiah?"' For he knew they had handed Him over because of envy."*
> —Matthew 27:15–17

Ultimately, Pilate had to ask, "What should I do?"

I agree with what psychologist William James once said: "When you have to make a choice and don't make it, that is in itself a choice." The choice one makes about Jesus is life's most important choice. "What will I do with Jesus?" is the question of questions. Pilate faced the question and made his decision. Even though he tried to clear himself with a ritual washing, this couldn't erase his blame.

> When Pilate saw that he was getting nowhere, but that a riot was starting instead, he took some water, washed his hands in front of the crowd, and said, "I am innocent of this man's blood. See to it yourselves.'"
> —Matthew 27:24

But it is never possible for anyone to say, "I wash my hands of all responsibility." Responsibility is something no one can wash away. God's call to salvation must be dealt with, and one simply cannot be a missional leader without dealing with this issue.

A Call to Service

God also calls the missional leader to His service. In the case of young Samuel, God called him to service though he was only 12. His service may have included caring for the lamps or some other kind of priestly assistance. God's call to enlistment does not come only to high-level prophets; people at all levels of experience and all ages are called to service. No one else can do exactly what God has purposed for you, but if He calls you to some specific task, don't doubt that task can get done without you. The problem is that your failure to answer the call may spoil God's first choice for your life. Remember the parable of the barren fig tree in the thirteenth chapter of the Gospel

> Failure to answer the call may spoil God's first choice for your life.

of Luke. It is clear this parable teaches that God wants His kingdom people to bear fruit (13:6–9): *"I have come looking for fruit on this fig tree and haven't found any. Cut it down! Why should it even waste the soil?"* (v. 7) And in the Gospel of John, the Lord says,

> *"You did not choose Me, but I chose you. I appointed you that you should go out and produce fruit and that your fruit should remain, so that whatever you ask the Father in My name, He will give you."*
> —John 15:16

Samuel had a clear calling from God, and so did Nehemiah. Every missional leader needs this clear sense of calling. With it, one's road toward missional leadership will be far stronger and far more confident. At first, many leaders did not feel they were capable of accomplishing what God had called them to do. Even Moses felt the same way when he shrank from the task at hand. *"But Moses replied to the LORD, 'I have never been eloquent—either in the past or recently or since You have been speaking to Your servant—because I am slow and hesitant in speech'"* (Exodus 4:10). The Apostle Paul wrote,

> *I came to you in weakness and fear, and with much trembling. My message and my preaching were not with wise and persuasive words, but with a demonstration of the Spirit's power, so that your faith might not rest on man's wisdom, but on God's power."*
> —1 Corinthians 2:2–5 (NIV)

It took some time for both Moses and Paul to stop worrying about the *medium* and begin concentrating on the *message*. They seemed to quake at the calling of God, and both had serious misgivings about their ability to carry out the special call of God on their lives. If we sometimes feel that way, let's keep in mind that humility is extremely important. We must recognize our own limitations. But we must never underestimate the power of God's enabling call. That is what missional leaders must always remember.

God is very kind in allowing us to be a part of His wonderful work. There is a story about a marriage feast in the Gospel of Luke. In this parable, Jesus describes our Father in terms of being a generous and gracious host who prepares a great feast for those responding to His invitation. Here is how the story goes:

> When one of those who reclined at the table with Him heard these things, he said to Him, "The one who will eat bread in the kingdom of God is blessed!"
>
> Then He told him: "A man was giving a large banquet and invited many. At the time of the banquet, he sent his slave to tell those who were invited, 'Come, because everything is now ready.'
>
> "But without exception they all began to make excuses. The first one said to him, 'I have bought a field, and I must go out and see it. I ask you to excuse me.'
>
> "Another said, 'I have bought five yoke of oxen, and I'm going to try them out. I ask you to excuse me.'
>
> "And another said, 'I just got married, and therefore I'm unable to come.'
>
> "So the slave came back and reported these things to his master. Then in anger, the master of the house told his slave, 'Go out quickly into the streets and alleys of the city, and bring in here the poor, maimed, blind, and lame!'
>
> "'Master,' the slave said, 'what you ordered has been done, and there's still room.'

"Then the master told the slave, 'Go out into the highways and lanes and make them come in, so that my house may be filled.'"
—Luke 14:15–23

There are several truths we need to learn from this great parable. God Himself has issued the invitation. His banquet is prepared and the doors to the feast are open. His kingdom is ready and waiting. Did you ever arrive home to hear your mother say that dinner would be ready when the rolls were done? The banquet God has prepared is always ready for those willing to respond to Him by faith.

God's invitation is the most extensive one ever offered. We are to extend out into the highways and hedges, and go to the uttermost parts of the earth with the good news of God's love.

God's invitation is inclusive. Everyone is included and anyone can respond.

God's invitation is intensive. Throughout the Bible, all people are invited to enjoy the blessings the Creator has prepared for us. The missional leader would like to see every individual in the world respond to Christ's gracious invitation.

God's invitation is expensive. The banquet has been prepared at the cost of Jesus Christ's sacrifice on the Cross. It is to the great redemptive banquet of God that we are to invite people. The missional leader has been chosen to be God's servant-inviter, just as the slave was sent out in the parable above. While we are to persuade people, we must never violate a person's individual freedom (2 Corinthians 5:11). We are to issue the invitation and present the intent of the Lord, but we are never to coerce, trick or over-persuade anyone to make an insincere commitment to God.

Ours is the privilege of being spokespeople for God. We are to be witnesses for Jesus Christ. Ours is the responsibility of inviting others to come to Jesus Christ, and this is not optional for Christians, especially for Christians who are missional leaders. We need to go out quickly, for opportunities pass swiftly. Time does not stand still. Yesterday is gone. Today is all we have, so the servant-inviter must seize opportunities without delay. The time will come when no one can work (John 9:4).

Some take up the mantle and some do not. Why do men and women leave home to spend their lives in a foreign country? Why would a skilled physician invest his life in a foreign country as a medical missionary to earn only a fraction of what he would earn at home? Why did pioneer missionaries George H. Lacey and his wife return to give the rest of their lives to Mexico after losing all 5 of their children in 15 days to scarlet fever contracted on the mission field? Why did William Carey go to India in 1792? Why did Lottie Moon go to China? We must be serious about responding to the call of being a missional leader, because it involves a ministry that takes us far beyond ourselves.

> The night will come when no one can work.
> —John 9:4

There is a story in the annals of the British Navy that on one occasion a destroyer was lying in a harbor of the West Indies, where five other ships of various nationalities were anchored. Suddenly a furious storm descended, with a wild, terrifying wind, and great eaves sweeping right into the harbor. What did the British captain do? He weighed anchor and steamed straight out to sea in the very teeth of the storm. Two days later he returned, battered but safe—and there were the other five ships lying piled up, wrecked upon the shore. It was their very refusal to face the seas and the storm, their clinging to security, which had been their undoing. Only the ship that ventured everything came through.

Another character from the Old Testament who had a clear calling from God was Gideon. God used Gideon in a powerful way. The selection of Gideon's army, however, left many in puzzlement. Many surrendered for service, but only some were selected, while the vast majority of the others were not. A terrific story to remember when we are questioning whether or not God can use us is the story of the selection of Gideon's army.

Jerubbaal (that is, Gideon) and everyone who was with him, got up early and camped beside the spring of Harod. The camp of Midian was north of them, below the hill of Moreh, in the valley.

The LORD said to Gideon, "You have too many people for Me to hand the Midianites over to you, or else Israel might brag: 'I did it myself.' Now announce in the presence of the people: 'Whoever is fearful and trembling may turn back and leave Mount Gilead.'" So 22,000 of the people turned back, but 10,000 remained.

Then the LORD said to Gideon, "There are still too many people. Take them down to the water, and I will test them for you there. If I say to you, 'This one can go with you,' he can go. But if I say about anyone, 'This one cannot go with you,' he cannot go." So he brought the people down to the water, and the LORD said to Gideon, "Separate everyone who laps water with his tongue like a dog. Do the same with everyone who kneels to drink." The number of those who lapped with their hands to

their mouths was 300 men, and all the rest of the people
knelt to drink water. The LORD said to Gideon, "I will
deliver you with the 300 men who lapped and hand the
Midianites over to you. But everyone else is to go home."
—Judges 7:1–7

Gideon and his army of only 300 men camped out prior to a battle with the Midianites and their allies. The task was enormous. They and their camels looked like a great swarm of locusts, and they entered the land to waste it. According to some, the Midianite army numbered around 135,000. This outmanned the Hebrew army by well over 100,000 warriors. If that weren't enough, Israel's army was drawn from an impoverished people, and they were hardly in fighting readiness.

The Hebrew army started out with 32,000 men, hardly enough even to challenge the 135,000 Midianites. But God said that 32,000 was too many, and He instructed Gideon to cut the number down. Then 22,000 men left because they were afraid. Of the 10,000 that remained, only those who, when they reached a brook before the battle, and did not allow themselves the time to kneel down and satisfy their thirst in the most convenient manner, were chosen. Rather, 300 of the men simply took up some water in their hands, to strengthen themselves for the battle, and then proceeded without delay. For Gideon's army, God chose only 300 men who weren't afraid, who were ready, and who were anxious to be about His bidding. The victory was won, the Midianite army was utterly destroyed, and God got the glory.

God is selecting His army even now. With a task so enormous, God wants many missional leaders—even though He could use a small number of people. But God cannot win victories with followers who are afraid, or who are attacking the wrong side. He can't win victories if His army is unprepared and anxious. He can if we are willing to become a part of victories with those who are unafraid. How about it?

Are you willing to become a part of God's army, knowing you may be tremendously outnumbered? You may sit regularly in a pew, but this does not mean you have taken your place in God's army. God's army requires real missional leaders

> **Are you willing to become a part of God's army?**

who are ready, willing, and anxious to be about the Father's business.

Don't say yes too quickly. You must count the cost. This involves sacrifice, change, and a willingness to work with others. Being open to this will take you well on your way to becoming a missional leader. Above all, a missional leader knows that God's call to service must be taken very seriously.

He Chose Us

It should have been no surprise that God's people won the victory over the Midianite army. But they have not always experienced such victories. Why? I think it is because too often we have disobeyed God's voice and ignored Christ's way. Will our generation experience the victory? Will we see God work? That is up to us. Will we follow Him? Will we take His power and use it? A husband and wife were discussing the possibility of taking a trip to the Holy Land. The husband asked, "Wouldn't it be fantastic to go to the Holy Land and stand and shout the Ten Commandments from Mount Sinai?" The wife answered, "It would be better if we stayed home and kept them."

On May 10, 2006, I received a phone call from a person I had never met or with whom I had never even spoken. At the request of several others, this person called to ask if I might consider allowing my name to be placed in nomination for the presidency of the Southern Baptist Convention. As God is my witness, having a top denominational position in the nationwide Convention had never crossed my heart or mind. Now, I had pondered the possibility of being the president of a state convention at some point. When the first call came asking me to consider the national Southern Baptist Convention presidency, however, I thought the caller was teasing. Later, I questioned his sanity!

> ## It had never crossed my heart or mind.

He asked me to at least begin praying about the possibility. I did begin to pray earnestly. Having a clear sense of purpose and calling for something of this magnitude was of extreme importance. I called friends and asked for their prayer and counsel. I searched the Scriptures daily to see if God might speak to me through His Word. I sought the fullness of the Holy Spirit in order to have a clear peace about this option. To be honest, for over a week I struggled and could not come to a sense of peace about whether or not this was a calling from God. Finally, almost ten days after that initial phone call, I finally felt a peace from God that I was to allow my name to be placed in nomination, even though I felt the nomination would lead to my certain defeat. I was well aware I lacked national exposure, but I did begin to sense God's call that there were important, key issues that needed to be discussed and considered in a positive way, and that I could possibly bring those issues to the fore.

With every belief I would lose the election, I moved forward with a clear sense of calling that the Lord wanted me to run for national office in the Convention. I knew what sacrifice this meant. For me, this was about as serious a decision as I have ever made; it was an irrecoverable moment. This crossroads opportunity increased my belief that God wanted me to be faithful to His calling—despite what I might think of it myself.

Still convinced of God's call to run but still convinced that my candidacy would end in defeat, I proceeded for the next few weeks until Convention time. The Convention was held in Greensboro, North Carolina, which ironically is my hometown. It was there where I had first felt God's call on my life. Being raised in a home without a spiritual foundation, I was thankful to be invited (by a godly couple) to a small Southern Baptist church not far from our home. As a young child, I began to find the church to be a place of God's love, a place of stability, and a place where God's Word was revered. Although my call to salvation came at age nine, my actual calling to ministry was expressed before that as a four-year-old boy during a Vacation Bible School commencement service. I let it be known that when I grew up I was going to be a preacher. That calling was so clear to my little heart that I never doubted it. In fact, I honestly have no conscious memory of a time I did not know what God wanted to do with my life.

The election as president of the Southern Baptist Convention did occur in Greensboro, North Carolina. The church where I made public my call to ministry and where my salvation occurred was less than a mile from the coliseum where the national Convention and the election took place. From the Convention hotel, one literally could see the steeple of the church building. The home where my family lived for several years was less than a hundred yards from the parking lot of the coliseum.

I awoke early on the morning of the election and began to study God's Word. By the way, I have read the Bible through every year since 1974. As I read the Gospel of John on the morning of June 13, I came to chapter 15, verse 16. That verse says, *"You did not choose Me, but I chose you. I appointed you that you should go out and produce fruit and that your fruit should remain."* I am not a mystic or a believer in happenstance, but most persons of faith can understand that there are times when one reads Scripture and knows that a particular verse speaks to his or her heart for a particular reason. At that moment, I knew God was speaking to me about the events of the day. In a time of prayer, I sensed God assuring me that the fruit He wished for me to bear for Him would be eternal in nature. I believed at that moment that the Lord was somehow arranging my election as president of my denomination. I knew that God's call would involve me in a way I had never anticipated. Because of the assurance of that morning, I was able to go through the day with relative calm, knowing what was going to happen. I am thankful the Lord gave me a little time to prepare for the press conference and the ensuing rush of events that followed the election.

God calls people to a variety of tasks. We may ignore His call, or we may accept it. Either way, a missional leader is a person of calling. The towering mountain peaks in the history of Christ's kingdom have been those who answered, *"Here I am. Send me"* to God's voice asking, *"Who should I send? Who will go for Us?"* (Isaiah 6:8). In the passage explored earlier, Samuel said yes to God and became a missional leader. As he matured, Samuel's reputation as God's spokesman spread throughout the land. When he said, "Thus says the Lord," you could be sure of the divine fulfillment of his messages. Many can say, "Thus says the Lord," but only the words of a true prophet were upheld by God. Just as the call came to Samuel, and as it came to Nehemiah, Moses, and Paul, so it comes to us, for many reasons, and in many ways.

In *Point Man,* Steve Farrar tells the story of George

McCluskey. When McCluskey married and started a family, he wanted his children to follow Christ. Farrar writes,

> "He decided to invest one hour each day in prayer for them. . . . After a time, he decided to expand his prayers to include not only his children, but their children and the children after them. Every day between 11 A.M. and noon, he would pray for the next three generations.
>
> As the years went by, McCluskey's two daughters committed their lives to Christ and married men who went into full-time [Christian] ministry. The two couples produced four girls and one boy. Each of the girls married a minister, and the boy became a pastor. The first two children born to this generation were both boys. Upon graduation from high school, the two cousins chose the same college and became roommates. During their sophomore year, one boy decided to go into the ministry as well. The other one didn't. He. . . .undoubtedly felt some pressure to continue the family legacy. . . .but he decided to pursue his interest in psychology."

Those whom God calls, God enables.

This boy earned a PhD degree and eventually wrote many books for parents that became best-sellers. He started a radio program "heard on more than a thousand stations each day," writes Farrar. The man's name: James Dobson.

Through his prayers, George McCluskey affected far more than one family. The call of God comes for salvation as well as to service. And those whom God calls, God enables.

Reflections

1. Do you think great leaders need to have a specific personality type? Why or why not?

2. Why is one's decision about Christ important? How would you have answered Pilate's question, *"What should I do then with Jesus?"*

3. What does the call to missional leadership involve? What is the cost?

CHAPTER 3

A Missional Leader
Is a Person of Vision

An Asian hermit lived in a remote village, tending his garden and spending much of his time in prayer. One day he thought he heard the voice of God telling him to go to Rome, so he obeyed, setting out on foot. Weary weeks later, he arrived in the city at the time of a great festival. The little monk followed the crowd surging down the streets into the Colosseum. He saw the gladiators stand before the emperor and say, "We who are about to die salute you." Then he realized these men were going to fight to the death for the entertainment of the crowd. He cried out, "In the name of Christ, stop!"

As the games began, he pushed his way through the crowd, climbed over the wall, and dropped to the floor of the arena. When the crowd saw the tiny figure rushing to the gladiators and saying, "In the name of Christ, stop!" They thought it was part of the show and began laughing. When they realized it wasn't a joke, the laughter turned to anger. As he was pleading with the gladiators to stop, one of them plunged a sword into his body. He fell to the sand. As he was dying, his last words were, "In the name of Christ, forbear (stop)!"

Then a strange thing happened. The gladiators stood looking at the tiny figure lying there. A hush fell over the Colosseum. Way up in the upper rows, a man stood and made his way to the exit. Others began to follow. In dead silence, everyone left the Colosseum.

The year was A.D. 391, and that was the last battle to the death between gladiators in the Roman Colosseum. Never again in the great stadium did men kill each other for the entertainment of the crowd, all because of one tiny voice that could hardly be heard above the tumult. One voice—one life—that spoke the truth in God's name. This early believer was a great example of a missional leader with vision. His courage, his conviction, and his calling are obvious, and by acting on the vision given to him by God, he brought about an incredibly important change.

Missional leaders have issues

Someone described a leader as a person who sees that which does not yet exist. Henry and Richard Blackaby, in their book *Spiritual Leadership*, say that a spiritual leader's task is to move people from where they are to where God wants them to be. That is influence. That is vision. Nehemiah showed the vision he held for the people:

> *After I made an inspection, I stood up and said to the nobles, the officials, and the rest of the people, 'Don't be afraid of them. Remember the great and awe-inspiring Lord, and fight for your countrymen, your sons and daughters, your wives and homes.'*
> —Nehemiah 4:14

Nehemiah's vision included an element of encouragement as he exhorted his people, *"Do not be afraid."* It contained an element of personal preparation. In his words, *"After I made an inspection."* It contained an element of divine presence when he said, *"Remember the great and awe-inspiring Lord."* It contained instruction as he admonished them to *"fight for your countrymen, your sons and your daughters, your wives and your homes."* His vision was multifaceted and it showed preparation and faith. Both elements are extremely important for the missional leader of vision.

Besides readiness and faith, there are several other issues for the missional leader that have an impact on vision. Two of them are credibility and sensitivity. Clyde Fant, in his book *Preaching for Today*, writes that credibility is "defined as the weight given to the assertions of a speaker and the acceptance accorded" those assertions by the hearers. Fant says credibility involves "two factors: trustworthiness and expertness...the greater the trustworthiness and expertness of the speaker, the greater [the] credibility."

> **The missional leader must be committed to the same selfless service as the Lord Jesus.**

But credibility is not as crucial as sensitivity. It is important that people see the missional leader not as an all-knowing, infallible source of information on all subjects, but rather as one who speaks with authority and passion.

Some leaders display dazzling mental acuity and yet almost unbelievable ignorance when it comes to relationships. The missional leader knows that one's sensitivity to people is far more difficult and important than adding facts to one's brain. The missional leader needs both credibility and sensitivity. The missional leader must be committed to the same selfless service as the Lord Jesus. Jesus Christ did not just model servant leadership—He *was* a servant as well as a leader. Missional leaders will follow the example of our Lord.

Another issue of extreme importance within the framework of vision is the issue of charisma. Every missional leader needs to be seen as a truly charismatic individual. I am not talking about some kind of charismatic theology, but about public persona where the individual is seen as *charismatic* in the best sense of the word. There are two basic characteristics that typify a missional leader with the sort of magnetism I am talking about. The charismatic leader is perceived as possessed by a purpose greater than himself or herself, an enthusiasm for life, composure under stress, and dedication to the goal of striking blows for the kingdom.

Could anyone deny the charisma of figures like Adolph Hitler, Mahatma Gandhi, Golda Meir, Martin Luther King Jr., or Nelson Mandela? These individuals, along with countless others in history, evidenced that kind of enthusiasm, composure under stress, and dedication to the goal. They were missional leaders with a vision. Whether for evil or for good, they were committed to the task at hand, and their life's purpose was greater than themselves.

Perhaps there is no better illustration of this commitment to principle and honor as a letter Major Sullivan Ballou of the Union army to his wife, Sarah, a week before the battle of Bull Run, July 14, 1861. They had been married only six years. These powerful words still touch the soul.

My Very Dear Sarah:

The indications are very strong that we shall move in a few more days—perhaps tomorrow. Lest I should not be able to write again, I feel impelled to write a few lines that may fall under your eye when I shall be no more....

I have no misgivings about or lack of confidence in the cause in which I am engaged, and my courage does not halt or falter. I know how strongly American civilization now leans on the triumph of the Government, and how great a debt we owe to those who went before us through the blood and suffering of the Revolution. And I am willing, perfectly willing, to lay down all my joys in this life to help maintain this Government and to pay that debt....

Sarah, my love for you is deathless: it seems to bind me with mighty cables that nothing but Omnipotence could break, and yet my love for country comes over me like a strong wind and bears me irresistibly on, with all these chains to the battlefield.

The memories of all the blissful moments I have spent with you come creeping over me, and I feel most deeply grateful to God, and you, that I have enjoyed them so long. And how hard it is for me to give them up and burn to ashes the hopes of future years, when, God willing, we might still have lived and loved together and seen our sons grown up to honorable manhood around us.

If I do not [return], my dear Sarah, never forget how much I love you, and when my last breath escapes me on the battlefield, it will whisper your name. Forgive my many faults and the many pains I have caused you. How thoughtless, how foolish I have often-times been....

O Sarah, if the dead can come back to this earth and flit unseen around those they loved, I shall always be near you in the gladdest day and in the darkest night, amidst your happiest scenes and gloomiest hours—always, always:

*and if there be a soft breeze upon your cheek, it shall by
my breath, or the cool air cools your throbbing temple,
it shall be my spirit passing by. Sarah, do not mourn me
dead: think I am gone, and wait for me, for we shall meet
again...*

Sullivan

Major Ballou was killed one week later at the first battle of
Bull Run. This story truly represents charisma in its finest
sense. Everyone can learn to be more charismatic in these ways.
Almost every missional leader I know truly believes that the
purpose they serve is greater than themselves. Certainly this
relates back to the issue of call, because if God places a call
upon a person's life, that person can be certain the purpose
of his or her life is far greater than his or her own physical
life. People follow a charismatic leader. This is not referring to
a blind, cultic following of a person, but the following of a
purpose which points beyond one's own self.

Perhaps one of the greatest examples of this kind of
visionary leadership is found in the Old Testament story of
King Saul, David, and Goliath. In the first Book of Samuel,
chapter seventeen, we see the story of Israel in its ongoing
struggle with the Philistines. It was a time of great trauma for
the Hebrew people.

*The Philistines were standing on one hill, and the
Israelites were standing on another hill with a ravine
between them. [Goliath] the Philistine said, "Send me
a man so we can fight each other." When Saul and all
Israel heard these words from the Philistine, they lost their
courage and were terrified.*
—1 Samuel 17:3,10–11

The twentieth chapter of 1 Chronicles records another time when Israel was at war with its perennial enemy. But something has changed dramatically. In this account, the Israelites were fearless. The Israelite Sibbecai killed a Philistine named Sippai. In yet another battle, Elhanan killed Lahmi, the brother of Goliath. And Jonathan, David's nephew, killed a giant who had a rather interesting anatomical anomaly—he had six fingers on each hand and six toes on each foot.

Why the difference in perspective and attitude between these two historical incidents? The key is realizing who the king was in each battle. In the first battle, Saul was king. He was no giant killer. In the second battle, the king was David. He was a giant killer. And when a giant killer leads, the followers want to take on giants too. Missional leaders need to set the pace and believe there is a purpose that gives courage, strength, and vision!

> **When a giant killer leads, the followers want to take on giants too.**

What was the key factor enabling David to have this vision, courage, and victory perspective? It was the true power of genuine charisma. David said to Goliath,

> *"You come against me with a dagger, spear, and sword, but I come against you in the name of the LORD of Hosts, the God of Israel's armies—you have defied Him. Today, the LORD will hand you over to me. Today, I'll strike you down, cut your head off....Then all the world will know that Israel has a God."*
> —1 Samuel 17:45, 46

David placed all his faith in the Lord God Almighty. Saul, on the other hand, put his faith in armor. He tried putting his on David thinking it would protect him. *"Then Saul had his own military clothes put on David. He put a bronze helmet on David's head and had him put on armor"* (1 Samuel 17:38). Soon David realized Saul's armor simply did not fit. That did not deter the young son of Jesse, for David did not put his faith in armor but rather in the God of Israel. Because he was a missional leader of great vision, he went out to face the giant. That was the charisma of David's life.

This young shepherd boy is an excellent example of charisma. David's charisma was not based on a personality type, educational attainment, environmental, or hereditary factors. His charisma was based on a vision from the Lord. He joins the great men and women of history who truly believed that God could call and that He would bless with a vision. Both David and Nehemiah show the missional leader to be a person of godly character, calling, and vision.

There is a Bible proverb that says, *"Without revelation, people run wild, but one who keeps the law will be happy"* (Proverbs 29:18). Another way to say this is, *"Where there is no vision, the people perish"* (KJV). A truer word can never be spoken. God's people are calling for visionary, missional leaders. The irrecoverable moment at which many churches, organizations, and denominations stand will be influenced positively only by men and women with a calling and a clear vision from God. Can you have that kind of vision? I believe every person holding this book can. You will, however, have to answer the same question Jesus put to Simon Peter:

> When they got out on land, they saw a charcoal fire there, with fish lying on it, and bread.
> *"Bring some of the fish you've just caught,"* Jesus told

them. So Simon Peter got up and hauled the net ashore, full of large fish—153 of them. Even though there were so many, the net was not torn.

"Come and have breakfast," Jesus told them. None of the disciples dared ask Him, "Who are You?" because they knew it was the Lord. Jesus came, took the bread, and gave it to them. He did the same with the fish.

This was now the third time Jesus appeared to the disciples after He was raised from the dead.

When they had eaten breakfast, Jesus asked Simon Peter, "Simon, son of John, do you love Me more than these?"

"Yes, Lord," he said to Him, "You know that I love You."

"Feed My lambs," He told him.

A second time He asked him, "Simon, son of John, do you love Me?"

"Yes, Lord," he said to Him, "You know that I love You."

"Shepherd My sheep," He told him.

He asked him the third time, "Simon, son of John, do you love Me?"

Peter was grieved that He asked him the third time, "Do you love Me?" He said, "Lord, You know everything! You know that I love You."

"Feed My sheep," Jesus said. "I assure you: When you were young, you would tie your belt and walk wherever you wanted. But when you grow old, you will stretch out your hands and someone else will tie you and carry you where you don't want to go." He said this to signify by what kind of death he would glorify God. After saying this, He told him, "Follow Me!"

—John 21:9–19

Jesus met His disciples on the beach where He had already prepared breakfast for them. The scene must have stirred Peter's memory and touched his conscience. Surely he was recalling that first catch of fish (Luke 5:1–11) and perhaps even the feeding of the 5,000 with bread and fish (John 6). It was at the close of the latter event that Peter gave his clear-cut witness of faith in Jesus Christ (John 6:66–69). It is good for us to remember the past. We may have something to confess.

How loving of Jesus to feed Peter before He dealt with his spiritual needs. He gave Peter the opportunity to dry off, get warm, satisfy his hunger, and enjoy personal fellowship. This is a good example for us to follow as we care for God's people. Certainly spiritual needs are more important than physical ones, but caring for the physical can prepare the way for spiritual ministry. Our Lord does not so emphasize the soul that He neglects the body.

Peter and his Lord had already met privately and no doubt discussed Peter's sins, but since Peter denied the Lord *publicly*, it was important that there be a public restoration. Sin can be dealt with only to the extent it is known. Private sins should be confessed privately, and public sins publicly. Since Peter had denied the Lord three times, Jesus asked him three personal questions. He also encouraged him by giving a threefold commission, thus restoring Peter to his ministry.

A Key Question

Today's disciple is confronted with the same question Jesus asked Peter. Note the question itself: *"Simon, son of John, do you love Me more than these?"* That could mean different things. Jesus may have been asking Peter, "Do you love me more than these material things?" This may have included his boat, net, and other possessions. Perhaps Jesus referred to Peter's job. But then Jesus could have been asking Peter, "Do you love me more than these other disciples do?" The Lord may have been looking back to that night when Peter told Him, *"Even if everyone runs away, I will certainly not!"* (Mark 14:29).

Can you answer the question as Peter did? He said, *"You know that I love You."* Do you love God enough to give your entire life, all that you have and all that you are? We are so afraid to give our lives to the Lord, afraid—with good reason— our lives will never be the same. It is difficult to give ourselves to Him because we do not believe that in giving ourselves to Christ we receive riches beyond compare.

> Can you answer the question as Peter did?

In June of 1995, I attended the US Army War College in Carlisle Barracks, Pennsylvania. While there I met a tall, athletic man who daily rode back to the hotel with me. As the week began, people began coming to him for his autograph. When I questioned him about this he said that he had played "a little ball in his life." When I asked him who he played for, he told me the Pittsburgh Steelers. When I asked him if he was "any good," he said, "Well, I guess I was OK." I later learned that he, John Stallworth, had been one of the leaders in the Pittsburgh Steelers winning four Super Bowl victories.

During the week I teasingly told him that I really didn't know much about professional football and unless he played for the Dallas Cowboys, it didn't really mean a whole lot to me! But I did ask him the most important question. I said to him, "John, all I want to know is, do you love Jesus?" He replied to me that he did indeed love Jesus and was actively involved in a local church in Huntsville, Alabama. He serves the Lord there and speaks in many other places giving his strong testimony of faith in Jesus. The question to him is the question to all of us: Do you love Jesus?

See how and why Jesus asked this question of Peter three times. In English, we have a difficult time expressing the question Jesus asked because Greek has several words for *love*, but English has only one. We often use the word *love* in various ways, but in English, there is only one meaning. As a child, did you ever send someone a note saying something like this? "I love you, do you love me? If so, drop your pencil on the floor." This is one way we use the word, but Peter and Jesus had a different concept entirely. Jesus twice asked Peter, *"Do you love* [agape] *me more than these?"* Peter completely misses the point, or avoids it, by using another word for *love* by saying, *"I love you* [phileo]." He insists that Christ knows that, in spite of Peter's conduct. He passes by the *"more than these."*

The third time Jesus asks the question, He picks up the word *phileo*, which Peter used and challenges that. *"Peter, do you love* [phileo] *me?"* By this time, Peter was cut to the heart. He said, *"You know everything! You know that I love You."* No doubt the fact that Jesus asked him three times reminded him he once denied Jesus three times in the early morning by the fire. John 18:27 says: *"Peter then denied it again. Immediately a rooster crowed."*

Peter was on his way to becoming a missional leader. Love brought Peter a task. Jesus told him to be a shepherd to His sheep. A shepherd leads the sheep, feeds them, and helps them grow. When we take it upon ourselves to lead those around us in the things of the Lord, to feed them on the truth of God's Word, and to help them grow in the Christian life, then we shall really see what love is all about. The resurrected Christ commissioned us to lead the lost to Him. *"But you will receive power when the Holy Spirit has come upon you, and you will be my witnesses in Jerusalem, in all Judea and Samaria, and to the ends of the earth"* (Acts 1:8).

God has called and commissioned us to disciple those around us. As a church, we have been woefully inadequate in equipping and training new believers. I guess we expect them to grow overnight by themselves. Leonard Ravenhill tells about a group of tourists visiting a picturesque village. They walked by an old man sitting beside a fence. In a rather patronizing way, one tourist asked, "Were any great men born in this village?" The old man replied, "Nope, only babies." We must do the work of shepherding the flock. Mature Christians are not born; we must disciple them. We must lead them to the resurrected Christ, and help them grow in His care.

> I guess we expect them to grow overnight by themselves.

Love brought Peter a task. It also brought to him a cross. Jesus told Peter he would die for Him. Great love always involves responsibility, sacrifice, and doing the work of God. Over and over Jesus said that if we love Him, we will keep His commandments.

Peter went on to prove his love for Christ. He became the leader of the early church at Jerusalem. It is amazing that despite his miserable performance in the past, he was not only forgiven, but reinstated to God's service. God forgives and wants to use each of us. He continues to let us prove our devotion and love for Him.

Answer the question Jesus asks you:

Do you love Me more than these?
Do you love Me?
Do you love Me?

Do not doubt that you, too, can become a missional leader. You can have as clear a vision as Nehemiah and David did. Or you can have a growing sense of vision, as did Peter. Sometimes it takes longer for vision to grow in some than in others. But it will grow and become clear if you stay at the task; maybe even today.

Reflections

1. Some describe a leader as one who sees things that do not yet exist. What does this mean for the missional leader?

2. What is an irrecoverable moment? Have you ever had one?

3. Why was David a missional leader?

4. Why was Saul not a missional leader?

CHAPTER 4

A Missional Leader
Is a Person of Christlike Concern

After an evening worship service in a church I used to pastor, I stopped to greet some church members who brought visitors with them. One visitor was a young mother with a very active four-year-old child. As I greeted this young family, the four-year-old asked, "Are you Jesus?" After I regained my composure, I assured the young man that I was not Jesus, although I did love Jesus very much. At this point he looked at me and said, "Well, if you see Him, would you please tell Him that my daddy uses bad words." I assured the young man that indeed I would be in contact with Jesus and I would be praying for his daddy that he would not use bad words anymore.

> The missional leader is a person who carries a deep burden.

Obviously, this little boy had a deep concern. Even at his young age, he carried a burden with him that he would share, even with a stranger.

The missional leader is a person who carries a deep burden. This certainly relates to the previous discussion of vision as well as call. Specifically, however, the burden is one that must be articulated carefully to one's constituency. The burden Nehemiah felt was powerfully illustrated when he said, *"When I heard these words, I sat down and wept. I mourned for a number of days, fasting and praying before the God of heaven"* (1:4). A missional leader feels deeply about the needs that are evident in one's place of ministry or one's sphere of influence. The missional leader is not removed. We are not of the world, but we are still in it.

How many times have we wept over the lost condition of our nation and world? How often have we mourned and fasted and prayed because of the deep division and ineffectiveness of our churches? How often have we wept over the lack of support for missions and evangelism?

Differing Signs

In my tenure as president of the Southern Baptist Convention, I have seen wonderful signs of hope, life, and victory. I saw missionaries weep over their people groups. At the same time, I must confess I have seen other instances that give me great concern. Within our own denomination, there are factions that have become so decidedly disparate that some groups will not fellowship or dialogue with one another. Major factions have developed between different theological groups; groups which differ in ecclesiology and methodology.

> Having differences is good, not bad.

Might I affirm that having differences is good, not bad. It simply reflects a diverse body of Christ and is, therefore, healthy. Some in this division are thwarting the prayer request of Jesus when He prayed, *"May they all be one, as You, Father, are in Me and I am in You. May they also be one in Us, so the world may believe You sent Me"* (John 17:21). The heart of God is grieved when brothers and sisters in Christ exhibit the disunity so often found in denominations, churches, parachurches, and other Christian relationships. A missional leader is deeply and profoundly burdened, because there can be no casual or surface attention to deep issues. Satan wants us to focus on the wrong burdens, the wrong issues.

In the 1920s, leaders of France were painfully aware that Germany's devastating victories in World War I could be repeated. Much thought was given to how to defend their country from a possible German attack. One of the generals, Marshall Pétain, approached the minister of war, André Maginot, about a massive engineering project to defend the eastern border of France. After much argument and discussion, the leaders were convinced, and the Maginot Line was built. It was a system of over 50 forts with hundreds of artillery emplacements and turrets connected by a vast system of tunnels. It enabled France to quickly organize a defense against a German attack. It was an absolute engineering marvel. It even had a pressurized air system to keep poison gas on the outside. Most military tacticians thought the Maginot Line could be held indefinitely. It ran from the Swiss border on the south to the Ardennes Forest in the north. Later after Belgium terminated its alliance with France, there was an attempt to extend the line through the Belgium border, but the forts built there were nowhere as strong or advanced as the ones on the German border.

In September of 1939, when Germany declared war on France's ally, Poland, France responded with a declaration of war against Germany. For months the German army simply sat on its side of the border, not advancing, and the French generals congratulated themselves on the Maginot Line's effectiveness. Then, in early May of 1940, Germany declared war on Belgium and Holland. France, expecting Germany to attempt to flank the forts to the north, moved the bulk of its army north toward Belgium to meet the incoming Germans. Instead, the Germans marched in force through the Ardennes Forest, which General Pétain had called "impenetrable." At his suggestion, the border with Germany was left unguarded and unfortified. With little resistance, the Germans easily pushed through and surrounded the main French army in Belgium while their advanced units pushed on to Paris. In less than one month, the country was taken by Germany. The formidable, technologically advanced Maginot Line was simply bypassed.

The Maginot Line is an arcane reminder of France's defeat in World War II. To military historians, it is a symbol of strategic stupidity. I believe our Enemy wants us to focus on the wrong things. Many Christian leaders fail from a ministry standpoint because they get caught up in pet projects or singular issues that do not represent the real needs of the people to whom they are called to minister. It is so easy to get sidetracked and focus our efforts in the wrong direction.

In order to avoid this disastrous error, the missional leader must follow the example of our Lord Jesus. For whom was Jesus burdened? Even Nehemiah's terrible burden for his people is greatly eclipsed as we read the New Testament accounts of Jesus's burden for all humanity. In a broad sense, His heart went out to the city of Jerusalem, and He said, *"Jerusalem, Jerusalem! The city who kills the prophets and stones those who are sent to her. How often I wanted to gather your children together, as a hen gathers her chicks under her wings, but you were not willing!"* (Luke 13:34). The heart of our Lord and Savior poured out for the people of Jerusalem and Israel.

His heart was broken as He realized their rejection of God's call would lead to their ultimate destruction.

One does not have to look far into the New Testament to see the example of Jesus and His burden for His disciples. This burden was expressed in many ways. One of the great examples is the twenty-second chapter of the Gospel of Luke, where the Master expressed a deep concern for His friend, Peter. He said, *"But I have prayed for you that your faith may not fail. And you, when you have turned back, strengthen your brothers"* (22:32). He knew Peter would go through a time of great testing, even to the point of denying Him. Despite this, Jesus's deep burden is shown in His expression of prayer support for Peter. Jesus loved all His disciples, and He was deeply concerned about their walk and their future service for Him.

The familiar story of Jesus and His friend Lazarus also portrays the Lord's deep burden for those close to Him. The shortest verse in the Bible illustrates such a deep burden when John 11:35 says, *"Jesus wept."* Many have pondered why He cried. Was He simply expressing deep sorrow for the hurt and pain of the sisters of Lazarus? Was He weeping because He knew He would bring Lazarus back to life, and knew the deep regret that Lazarus would have not being able to stay in heaven? However we read that verse, do we cry over our people like that? Do we express that kind of deep responsibility for the lost around us?

The missional leader has a Christlike love for people. Nehemiah wrote,

> *The governors who preceded me had heavily burdened the people, taking food and wine from them, as well as a pound of silver. Their subordinates also oppressed the people, but I didn't do this, because of the fear of God.*
> —Nehemiah 5:15

Nehemiah had every right to extract some form of payment from the people. But his loving care and concern was exhibited throughout the letter. Also, his fear of God kept him from doing what was inappropriate. The spiritual fruit which Galatians 5:22–23 commands all of us to have contains the attribute of love. In fact, the list begins with love, then goes on to joy, peace, patience, kindness, goodness, faith, gentleness and self-control.

A word of caution, however. There are some burdens that arise out of wrong motives at this point. A powerful example of this is found in 2 Kings:

> *Four men with skin diseases were at the entrance to the gate. They said to each other, "Why just sit here until we die? If we say, 'Let's go into the city,' we will die there because the famine is in the city, but if we sit here, we will also die. So now, come on. Let's go to the Arameans' camp. If they let us live, we will live; if they kill us, we will die."*
>
> *So the diseased men got up at twilight to go to the Arameans' camp. When they came to the camp's edge, they discovered that there was not a [single] man there, for the Lord had caused the Aramean camp to hear the sound of chariots, horses, and a great army. The Arameans had said to each other, "The king of Israel must have hired the kings of the Hittites and the kings of Egypt to attack us." So they had gotten up and fled at twilight abandoning their tents, horses, and donkeys. The camp was intact, and they had fled for their lives.*
>
> *When these men came to the edge of the camp, they went into a tent to eat and drink. Then they picked up the silver, gold, and clothing and went off and hid them. They came back and entered another tent, picked [things]*

up, and hid them. Then they said to each other, "We're not doing what is right. Today is a day of good news. If we are silent and wait until morning light, we will be punished. Let's go tell the king's household."

The diseased men went and called to the city's gatekeepers and told them, "We went to the Aramean camp and no one was there—no human sounds. There was nothing but tethered horses and donkeys, and the tents were intact." The gatekeepers called out, and [the news] was reported to the king's household.

So the king got up in the night and said to his servants, "Let me tell you what the Arameans have done to us. They know we are starving, so they have left the camp to hide in the open country, thinking, 'When they come out of the city, we will take them alive and go into the city.'"

But one of his servants responded, "Please, let [messengers] take five of the horses that are left in the city. [The messengers] are like the whole multitude of Israelites who will die, so let's send them and see."

[The messengers] took two chariots with horses, and the king sent them after the Aramean army, saying, "Go and see." So they followed them as far as the Jordan. They saw that the whole way was littered with clothes and equipment the Arameans had thrown off in their haste. The messengers returned and told the king.

—2 Kings 7:3–15

It was a day of good news for these four lepers who were in such a terrible situation. Indeed, the situation for Israel as a whole was desperate. Because of the siege, the famine was great. Prices for food had gone through the ceiling. The situation reached such horrible levels that some people even resorted to cannibalism.

The lepers, even in normal circumstances, were extremely badly treated. These men, separated from human society according to law, and being at the point of starvation because of the circumstances, resolved to go to the Arameans for help. They reasoned they had nothing to lose. What they didn't know was that God had miraculously intervened on behalf of the people of Israel. God caused the enemy to flee after hearing the sounds of chariots and horses and a great army. The Arameans left, leaving behind all their wealth, equipment, and food. As the lepers approached the camp, they found it empty! The enemy who had been on the verge of victory was now gone. Talk about a dream come true! The lepers, who had nothing, now seemed to have everything. These men who had lost all hope now had everything they ever wanted.

Giving Away the Good News

> At some point in our lives we were starving spiritually, yet someone led the way to the Bread of life.

This story parallels our experience. Disciples of Jesus Christ have discovered the good news in a way similar to the four lepers discovering their booty. At some point in our lives we were starving spiritually, yet someone led the way to the Bread of life. We were lost in our sins, and then we discovered a way out of darkness into light. *"For God loved the world in this way: He gave His One and Only Son, so that everyone who believes in Him will not perish but have eternal life"* (John 3:16).

We know the people in northern Israel were in tremendous, almost unbelievable need. They were dying of starvation. They were resorting to the most dreadful kind of behavior.

Meanwhile, the lepers were going on a binge, having a big party, and enjoying the riches in the Aramean camp—and failing to share the wealth with others. What they couldn't consume, they hoarded.

Perhaps there is a parallel in this story for us because we, too, have hoarded the Good News. We have failed to share the spiritual wealth we have discovered. Individually, we have lost the zeal of our early faith. Corporately, the church has failed in reaching out to a lost and dying world. We enjoy what we have discovered in Christ, but we fail to do all we can to share the wealth. In England in 1792, a church official who was discussing William Carey's desire to be a missionary said, "Brother Carey is sincere enough, but I fear he has fallen into the hands of fanatics. Imagine us sending missionaries to the heathen! He will do it without our help!" Often, we, too, are as misled as the official. We won't share the blessing, but we do like to come to church and be blessed ourselves.

These lepers in 2 Kings came to recognize their duty to others. They resolved to do what they should have done before, because they knew what they were doing was wrong. They decided to go and tell the king the good news that the enemy had fled. This was a wonderful resolve, because we can rejoice every time anyone shares the good news with someone else. Why did the lepers decide to share? Was it out of great compassion? Were they worried about the welfare of others who had ostracized them for years? I doubt it.

The key to understanding their sudden altruism is found in verse 9: *"We're not doing what is right. Today is a day of good news. If we are silent and wait until morning light, we will be punished. Let's go tell the king's household."* They were afraid, and they shared the news because of fear and perceived suffering. They were compelled to share because they knew they couldn't get away with hoarding this good news.

This was a less-than-positive motive, but there are times our burden does come from guilt, fear, or duty. Why do you want to be a missional leader? Is there some motive that might bring about a burden that is less than godly? To be a missional leader of Christlike concern, we need to question our motives when we do a spiritual inventory. Nehemiah had a deep burden for the people that was appropriate. Our Lord Jesus gave us great examples of burdens for people, but with correct motive.

> We need to question our motives when we do a spiritual inventory.

When the Lord cared for burdens, He did it in ways His culture may not have found acceptable. He expressed deep compassion and concern for women, who in that day and time were so oppressed and marginalized. In a culture that prohibited a man from touching a woman, Jesus put His hands on a woman who was disabled by a spirit. *"Immediately she straightened up and praised God"* (Luke 13:13). In the fourth chapter of John, Jesus shows His burden not only for a woman, but for a Samaritan woman. He offered her the great gift of eternal life. *"But whoever drinks from this water that I will give him will never be thirsty again—ever! In fact, the water I will give him will become a well of water springing up within him for eternal life"* (4:14). In the Gospel of Matthew, Jesus tested a woman's faith, and He even teased her at the end of their dialogue.

> *When Jesus left there, He withdrew to the area of Tyre and Siden. Just then a Canaanite woman from that*

region came and kept crying out, "Have mercy on me, Lord, Son of David! My daughter is cruelly tormented by a demon."

Yet He did not say a word to her. So his disciples approached Him and urged Him, "Send her away because she cries out after us."

He replied, "I was sent only to the lost sheep of the house of Israel."

But she came, knelt before Him, and said, "Lord, help me!"

He answered, "It isn't right to take the children's bread and throw it to their dogs."

"Yes, Lord," she said, "yet even the dogs eat the crumbs that fall from their masters' table!" Then Jesus replied to her, "Woman, your faith is great. Let it be done for you as you want." And from that moment her daughter was cured.

—Matthew 15: 21–28

Who should missional leaders truly be concerned about? Jesus of course was concerned for everyone, but He focused His attention on especially needy groups of people. He was deeply concerned for those within His inner circle. He also expressed deep concern and burdens for His friends. He expressed deep compassion and concern for women, as shown above. Perhaps one of the greatest examples of Jesus's missional leadership is how He was concerned for and related to children. The gospel records Jesus's ministry to children whom He dearly loved.

Some people were bringing little children to Him so He might touch them, but His disciples rebuked them. When Jesus saw it, He was indignant and said to them, "Let the children come to Me. Don't stop them, for the kingdom of

God belongs to such as these. I assure you: Whoever does not welcome the kingdom of God like a little child will never enter it." After taking them in his arms, He laid His hands on them and blessed them.
—Mark 10:13–16

Missional leaders will follow the example of Jesus by showing Christlike concern for and paying particular attention to precious children.

Another particular burden Jesus felt was for the poor and the needy. Today, most of us see the poverty-stricken as those to whom we minister on a missions trip. But Jesus did not see the poor and lowly as a missions trip, but as constant companions and a consistent burden of everyday life. This is how we are to give to the needy among us:

"So whenever you give to the poor, don't sound a trumpet before you, as the hypocrites do.... But when you give to the poor, don't let your left hand know what your right hand is doing, so that your giving may be in secret. And your Father who sees you in secret will reward you."
—Matthew 6:2,3–4

There are many examples in Scripture where the Lord encourages us to give to the poor. *"'If you want to be perfect,' Jesus said to him, 'go, sell your belongings and give to the poor'"* (Matthew 19:21). This is a ministry the missional leader will never neglect.

Nehemiah had a keen sense of social justice. He dealt with the situation where the nobles and officials exacted usury from their own countrymen and caused great hardship on the people. *"What you are doing isn't right,"* Nehemiah told them. *Shouldn't you walk in the fear of our God [and not invite] the reproach of our foreign enemies?"* When corrected by Nehemiah, the people replied, *"We will return [these things] and require nothing more from them. We will do as you say"* (Nehemiah 5:9,12).

Nehemiah's concern for the poor and hurting was not only exhibited in the way he corrected the unjust nobles and officials, but also in the way he behaved personally. Seeing that the governors preceding him had placed heavy burdens upon the people, he made sure in his personal life no such event occurred. His social conscience was his ethical behavior, all based in reverence for God. *"The governors . . . oppressed the people, but I didn't do this, because of the fear of God"* (Nehemiah 5:15).

It is extremely important that missional leaders understand a burden for the lost must be paramount. In the Lord's Prayer, Jesus prays not only for the believers who had already come to Him, but also *"I pray not only for these, but also for those who believe in Me through their message"* (John 17:20). Do we have a deep concern for those who have not yet come to Christ? Are our hearts burdened for the lost? A missional leader will bear such a burden.

The fifteenth chapter of the Book of Luke tells of God's burden for the lost through the parables of the lost sheep, the lost coin, and the lost son. In each example, the Lord shows a burden for those needing to come home. Do we as missional leaders have the same kind of burden for those lost in salvation and service? It is easy to get sidetracked and focus only on those responding quickly to the gospel message. But are we missional people of deep concern and burden enough to adopt the attitude of Jesus for all who are lost?

The Apostle Paul likewise gave us a great example of developing and maintaining friendships and influencing people for the sake of Christ. The Apostle Paul displayed a deep love for those with whom he worked. Missional leaders should manifest that same kind of leadership characteristic. First Thessalonians 2:1–19 is a text demonstrating how Paul lived out this missional leadership characteristic.

For you yourselves know, brothers, that our visit with you was not without result. On the contrary, after we had previously suffered and been outrageously treated in Philippi, as you know, we were emboldened by our God to speak the gospel of God to you in spite of great opposition. For our exhortation didn't come from error or impurity or an intent to deceive. Instead, just as we have been approved by God to be entrusted with the gospel, so we speak, not to please men, but rather God, who examines our hearts. For we never used flattering speech, as you know, or had greedy motives—God is our witness—and we didn't seek glory from people, either from you or from others. Although we could have been a burden as Christ's apostles, instead we were gentle among you, as a nursing mother nurtures her own children. We cared so much for you that we were pleased to share with you not only the gospel of God but also our own lives, because you had become dear to us. For you remember our labor and hardship, brothers. Working night and day so that we would not burden any of you, we preached God's gospel to you. You are witnesses, and so is God, of how devoutly, righteously, and blamelessly we conducted ourselves with you believers. As you know, like a father with his own children, we encouraged, comforted, and implored each one of you to walk worthy of God, who calls you into His own kingdom and glory.

Also, this is why we constantly thank God, because when you received the message about God that you heard from us, you welcomed it not as a human message, but as it truly is, the message of God, which also works effectively in you believers. For you, brothers, became imitators of God's churches in Christ Jesus that are in Judea, since you have also suffered the same things from people of your own country, just as they did from the Jews. They killed both the Lord Jesus and the prophets, and persecuted us; they displease God, and are hostile to everyone, hindering us from speaking to the Gentiles so that they may be saved. As a result, they are always adding to the number of their sins, and wrath has overtaken them completely.

But as for us, brothers, after we were forced to leave you for a short time [in person, not in heart], we greatly desired and made every effort to return and see you face to face. So we wanted to come to you—even I, Paul, time and again—but Satan hindered us. For who is our hope, or joy, or crown of boasting in the presence of our Lord Jesus at His coming? Is it not you?
—1 Thessalonians 2:1–19

We so often fail in this way. I agree with one author who said there is little chance for people to get together as long as most of us want to be in the front of the bus, the back of the church, and the middle of the road!

We need authentic love

This Scripture tells us that relating to others, reaching out to others, must start with love. Agape love is the key to Paul's approach: *"We cared so much for you that we were pleased to share with you not only the gospel of God but also our own lives, because you had become dear to us."* "Dear" is a translation of the Greek word, *agape*, which means God's love. God's love is without limit, without end, and without condition. Paul's letter to Thessalonica illustrates the vital nature of love as it is reflected in Paul's life of leadership. These same qualities must be seen in our lives if we are to become missional leaders.

Our love must be authentic, as was Paul's. He did not use guile or trickery to win converts. He was not "baiting a hook." In other words, Paul did not trap people the way a clever salesman traps people into buying things. Spiritual witnessing and "Christian salesmanship" are different. Salvation does not lie at the end of a clever argument or a subtle presentation. It is a result of God's Word and the power of the Holy Spirit!

Paul's enemies in Thessalonica accused him of being a cheap peddler of this new message. They said that his only motive was to make money. In describing himself as a faithful steward, Paul answered these critics and Paul's readers knew he told the truth. Paul's time was noted for roaming philosophers, sorcerers, and other peddlers who used tricks to impress their audiences. But Paul approached the Thessalonians with honesty and an absence of deception and manipulation. He was honest, direct, and decisive. These are the marks of a missional leader!

Paul's enemies were attacking him on many fronts, including the charge of sexual impurity, a sin so prevalent among the traveling religious leaders of the day. Paul disclaimed anything of this type as a motive for his activities. He was sincere and authentic in his love and in his motive for ministry. There were no undercover reasons for his activities. He loved the people, and they sensed that. People sense the same resolve from present-day missional leaders.

There is an oft told story of a little boy whose sister needed a blood transfusion. The doctor explained she had the same disease the boy had recovered from two years earlier. Her only chance for recovery was a transfusion from someone who had previously conquered the disease. Since the two children had the same rare blood type, the boy was the ideal donor. "Would you give your blood to Mary?" the doctor asked. Johnny hesitated. His lower lip began to tremble. Then he smiled and said, "Sure, for my sister." Soon the two children were wheeled into the hospital room. Neither spoke, but when their eyes met, Johnny grinned. As the nurse inserted the needle into his arm Johnny's smile faded. He watched the blood flow through the tube. With the ordeal almost over, his voice, slightly shaking, broke the silence. "Doctor, when do I die?" Only then did the doctor realize why Johnny had hesitated, why his lip had trembled when he had agreed to donate his blood. He thought giving up his blood to his sister meant giving up his life. In that brief moment, he had made his great decision. This little boy's love was truly authentic. Is ours? A missional leader will have an authentic love.

> Our love must be authentic as well as gentle.

Our love must be authentic as well as gentle. First Thessalonians 2:7 says, *"Although we could have been a burden as Christ's apostles, instead we were gentle among you, as a nursing mother nurtures her own children."* Paul and his assistants were anything but authoritarian. They put aside their rights to being respected as Christ's apostles and to playing a dominating part. Instead, they demonstrated a gentleness and tenderness comparable to that of a mother nursing her own children.

Paul made personal sacrifices and cared for new converts himself. He had patience with new believers, and His love was gentle and risky. Our love must also be risky and self-giving. Paul said they had not only shared the gospel of God, but their lives as well. *"We cared so much for you that we were pleased to share with you not only the gospel of God but also our own lives, because you had become dear to us"* (1 Thessalonians 2:8).

Missional leaders invest their lives in the people around them. Is our love like that? It is difficult for many of us to love with that kind of absolute love. David Smith writes in his book, *The Friendless American Male*,

> Within each man there is a dark castle with a fierce dragon to guard the gate. The castle contains a lonely self, a self most men have suppressed, a self they are afraid to show. Instead they present an armored knight—no one is invited inside the castle. The dragon symbolizes the fears and fantasies of masculinity, the leftover stuff of childhood.

This is true for many of us, but self-giving, risky love requires a great commitment. Missional leaders love that way.

The Maginot Line, mentioned earlier, was an historical incident portraying unparalleled strategic stupidity. Many leaders could be great, missional leaders if they realized the strategic moves the Enemy makes to take away the burdens we should share with Christ.

Reflections

1. What was Nehemiah's burden?

2. Have we hoarded the good news and failed to share the spiritual wealth? How?

3. What is the essential message of the parables of the lost sheep, the lost coin, and the lost son?

CHAPTER 5

A Missional Leader
Is a Person of Spiritual Fruitfulness

During the pre-Revolutionary time when the United States was still a British colony, a man named Edward Braddock arrived in Virginia as commander in chief of British forces in America. War with France was on. His task against the French was simple, or so he thought. After taking Fort Duquesne, he told Benjamin Franklin, in two or three days he would proceed to capture the French fort at Niagara, and if winter did not come too soon, he would take Frontenac as well. It all sounded so easy.

Franklin cautioned Braddock about the danger of ambushes from the natives along the nearly four-mile-long line. Braddock replied, "These savages may indeed be a formidable enemy to your raw American militia, but upon the king's regular and disciplined troops, sir, it is impossible they should make any impression." Even George Washington, Braddock's aide-de-camp, found reasoning with the general useless. Braddock refused to take defensive measures and fight the Canadian French and their native allies as they should be fought. At about 10:00 A.M. on July 8, 1755, the British forces were attacked near present-day Pittsburgh. The battle was a disaster for the

British. The enemy took 977 casualties out of 1,469 troops, two-thirds of their men. Braddock was mortally wounded and died a few days later. The heaviest losses were to the Virginia Militia under George Washington's command. Only 33 men out of three American companies survived. It is fair to say they underestimated the enemy.

We are a new creation

Negative consequences always follow when we underestimate our enemies. For Christians, too, there is an Enemy. Satan is a master strategist, and he is winning battles right and left. You do not need to be reminded of the statistics regarding family failures, moral breakdown, church failures, international strife, terrorism, and so on. He is so good at being bad. If one allowed oneself, you could despair at the recognition of Satan's victories. Much like Braddock, we have become arrogant to the point we fail to see, or even to look for, reality.

We have deeply misunderstood the power of the Enemy. We have underestimated his impact on our lives, even upon our leadership capabilities. He has distracted us so often by making us fight the wrong battles and focus on the wrong burdens. A missional leader is a person of Christlike spiritual fruitfulness. This is expressed in many different ways. A missional leader should have the kind of selfless character that Nehemiah exhibited: *"I didn't demand the food allotted to the governor, because the burden on the people was so heavy"* (5:18). In New Testament terms, that shows a Christlike spirit. Jesus did not *model* a servant spirit, He *was* a servant.

It was an integral part of who He was, not something He sought to display only on occasion. It was at the core of who He was.

One of the great surprises of being president of my denomination has been the amount of contact I have had with various secular politicians at the highest level. Amazingly, many have sought time with me for various reasons. To be invited to the Oval Office to visit with the President of the United States is an exciting and humbling experience. To pray hand in hand with the President is an awesome experience! And various other officials have come for advice on all sorts of matters.

During a political campaign season, one hears a great deal about the characteristics of character, integrity, honesty, and value systems. There is a great deal of discussion about how much character actually does matter to the US population. Some honestly feel that character is not nearly as important as it once was. In fact, I have to agree with that assessment. Generally, people today do not seem to care nearly as much as they once did. So should character matter? The answer is yes; it should matter very much, especially among God's people. Embarrassing, highly public failings have called all evangelicals to renewed understanding of character and integrity among Christian leaders.

> **Character should matter very much, especially among God's people.**

There is much written today about leadership from a business perspective. While there are many parallels between competent leadership in the business world and the world of ministry, there are some things we should emphasize to an even greater extent in the church. I am talking about missional leadership. A question not usually asked in leadership studies is, "How do leaders exhibit the fruits of the Spirit?" A true missional leader will be a person of integrity and character who exhibits the fruits of the Spirit. The Bible identifies the fruits of the Spirit as love, joy, peace, patience, kindness, goodness, faithfulness, gentleness, and self-control (Galatians 5: 22–23).

How is that fruit exhibited in our lives? In this and the following chapters, we will see the ways this fruit is borne out in the life of the missional leader.

I mentioned earlier that people expect many leaders to be very aggressive, strategically adept, incredibly persistent, and sometimes even super intelligent. The example of our Lord Jesus shows true missional leadership and the living out of the fruits of the Spirit. His leadership was powerful and the followship was incredible. This occurred because of His ability to show the love of God, the joy of God, the peace of God, and the patience of God in a powerful and influential way. Missional leaders should seek the spiritual fruit God grants to each genuine believer, because the fruit of the Spirit is the primary descriptor of missional leadership. Spiritual fruit is important beyond words. This fruit is not possible in the life of a leader who is outside the kingdom of God.

John's third chapter tells of Jesus's interview with Nicodemus. He says, *"You must be born again."* New life in Christ is like birth. There are two things brought about in physical birth. First, it fixes one's nature. When a baby is born, parents do not become alarmed and apprehensive for fear the baby will turn into a little monkey. They know that human nature is fixed by birth. Birth also fixes one's relations. A child is the offspring of parents. He or she may not always act like a child of the parents. Perhaps the child may run away or otherwise dishonor the name of the parents, but that child is still their child, because this relationship is fixed by birth.

In the same way, our spiritual nature is fixed by new birth in Jesus Christ. When we are born again, we become individuals with the Spirit of God living within us. This makes us different from the people we used to be, and different from those who do not know Christ. We are possessed of a new nature. The Bible says we are a new creation. Therefore, we think differently, and our nature changes. *"But to all who did receive Him, He gave them the right to be children of God, to those who believe in His name"* (John 1:12). Our relationships change as well. We are part of a new family, the family of God, and our relationship is fixed as the child of our heavenly Father. This brings great security.

The Apostle Paul says, we are *"justified by faith in Jesus Christ"* (Galatians 2:16). Justification or being made right in the sight of God is an experience that takes place once and for all. It is never repeated simply because it does not need repeating. It brings one into a new relation with God that is never reversible. Forgiveness and many other things need repeating in the life of a Christian, because sin breaks our fellowship with God, just as disobedience breaks a child's fellowship with his parents. But the sinner who has been justified never again comes under the condemnation of the law. Therefore, there is no need for justification again. In the Gospel of John, Jesus says, *"I assure you: Anyone who hears My word and believes Him who sent me has eternal life and will not come under judgment but has passed from death to life"* (5:24). The Apostle Paul enumerates the things that might be thought able to separate one from the love of God. Then he concludes by saying none of these or anything else can do so.

> *No, in all these things we are more than victorious through Him who loved us. For I am persuaded that neither death nor life, nor angels nor rulers, nor things present, nor things to come, nor powers, nor height, nor depth, nor any other created thing will have the power to separate us from the love of God that is in Christ Jesus our Lord!*
> —Romans 8:37–39

As we consider spiritual fruit in the life of the missional leader, let me be very clear. While there are things a believer in Christ cannot lose, there are things one definitely can lose, such as compassion, fellowship, a willing spirit, and a clean heart.

Be gracious to me, God,
* according to Your faithful love;*
* according to Your abundant compassion,*
* blot out my rebellion.*
Wash away my guilt,
* and cleanse me from my sin.*
For I am conscious of my rebellion,
* and my sin is always before me.*
Against You—You alone—I have sinned
* and done this evil in Your sight.*
So You are right when You pass sentence;
* You are blameless when You judge.*
Indeed, I was guilty [when I] was born;
* I was sinful when my mother conceived me.*
Surely You desire integrity in the inner self,
* and You teach me wisdom deep within.*
Purify me with hyssop, and I will be clean;
* wash me, and I will be whiter than snow.*
Let me hear joy and gladness;
* let the bones You have crushed rejoice.*
Turn Your face away from my sins
* and blot out all my guilt.*
God, create a clean heart for me
* and renew a steadfast spirit within me.*
Do not banish me from Your presence
* or take Your Holy Spirit from me.*
Restore the joy of Your salvation to me,
* and give me a willing spirit.*

Then I will teach the rebellious Your ways,
*   and sinners will return to You.*
Save me from the guilt of bloodshed, God,
*   the God of my salvation,*
*   and my tongue will sing of Your righteousness.*
Lord, open my lips,
*   and my mouth will declare Your praise.*
You do not want a sacrifice, or I would give it;
*   You are not pleased with a burnt offering.*
The sacrifice pleasing to God is a broken spirit.
*   God, You will not despise a broken and humbled heart.*
—Psalm 51:1–17

We can lose close fellowship with our Lord when unconfessed sin is present in the life of the believer. The sad truth is that many live much of their lives like this. Instead of dealing with the root problem, they live a life that is miserable, bitter, and unfulfilled. They begin to find fault in everyone else. Instead of dealing honestly, we establish a pattern of dishonesty before God.

When King Frederick II, an eighteenth-century King of Prussia, was visiting a prison in Berlin, the inmates tried to prove to him how they had been unjustly imprisoned. All except one. That one sat quietly in a corner, while all the rest protested their innocence. Seeing him sitting there oblivious to the commotion, the king asked him why he'd been imprisoned.

"Armed robbery, Your Honor."

The king asked, "Were you guilty?"

"Yes, Sir," he answered. "I entirely deserve my punishment."

The king then gave an order to the guard, "Release this guilty man. I don't want him corrupting all these innocent people."

Experiencing Intimacy and Fruitfulness

Have you lost sweet closeness with the Lord? The words of Jesus in Matthew are sobering: *"These people honor me with their lips, but their heart is far from Me"* (15:8). This involves a serious loss, the loss of the Holy Spirit's fullness and, therefore, divine direction.

> When we are right with God, we have a major and positive impact on a lost world.

We can lose the joy of salvation. When the fellowship with the Lord is gone, so is the joy. Worship becomes hollow. Working for the Lord becomes work. We find ourselves seeking entertainment instead of instruction. We lose the wonder of life.

We can lose our influence. When we are right with God, we have a major and positive impact on a lost world. But when we have lost close companionship with God, which is the sharp edge of being upright with the Lord, then we lose our ability to be salt and light in our world. We justify our ungodly behavior by stating, "We're only human," while our world suffers and goes to hell.

I earlier mentioned the parable of the fig tree from the Gospel of Luke (13:6–9). This tree illustrates the reality that many believers, some I'm afraid who wish to become missional leaders, have lost their influence because they have lost the fruit of the Spirit. Though they still may belong to the Lord as His children, they do not exhibit the fruit of the Spirit and therefore cannot lead as effectively as God would wish. What happened in the story of the fig tree?

There are certain facts about this fig tree that demand our attention. It was a planted tree. That means this tree is not a child of chance. It is not where it is because some passing breeze has happened to drop a seed upon this particular spot. It is there because someone possessed of intelligence had planted it there. This is also true with Christians. God has a plan for every life, a truth enforced over and over again throughout the Bible. Jesus tells us God gives a special commission to every person. In speaking to His own disciples, the Lord said, *"As the Father has sent Me, I also send you"* (John 20:21*b*). God planned our lives just as He did the life of Jesus.

The purpose of this fig tree was to bear fruit. It was to give an account of itself in terms of figs. It was not in this place of privilege and opportunity just for itself. It was there to serve. That also is the purpose of our being here. God never planned that any person should live for himself or herself. He never designed any life to be useless or hurtful. We are not here to lean, but to lift; not to hinder, but to help. The fact that God has put every one of us here for a helpful purpose means that helpfulness is within our reach, and we can be of genuine service if we will.

This fig tree was planted in a vineyard. That is, it was planted in a place of peculiar privilege. It was in possession of special opportunities. That, too, is the case with so many of us. Maybe we may have been born with the moral momentum of a pious ancestry flowing in our veins. We may have enjoyed the shelter of a Christian home. We all are part of a nation saturated in some measure by Christian ideals. We all have had the privileges of the open Bible and the open church. These things increase our obligation to be of service to others.

In spite of the fact that this tree was planted in a place of special privilege where fruit was to be rightfully expected, it utterly failed to fulfill the purpose for which it was planted. When the owner came in search of fruit he found none. He came again only to be disappointed. No wonder he ordered it cut down! It refused to fulfill the purpose for which it had been planted, cultivated, and protected. And, in an analogous way, failure is possible for us. The fact that God plans our lives does not mean He will compel us to carry out His plan. He has dreamed great dreams for every one of us, but we may fail, thwart, and disappoint Him. Day after day God comes, seeking some worthy fruit at our hands, and finds none. We refuse to enter into His holy and gracious purpose for our lives. He looks for the fruit of a missional leader and often finds none.

Examine the results of such failure. The first obvious result is uselessness. This fruitless tree was a thing of no use. And that is the tragic truth about so many, both in the church and out of it. They are guilty of no vicious or outrageous wrongdoing. They do not violate the law. They are just utterly ineffectual and absolutely useless. They hear the call of great needs ringing in their ears. but they never seem to care. What a tragic loss. I am convinced the most appalling waste that afflicts the church today is the complacent moral and spiritual uselessness of so many decent and capable Christians.

And this waste is not simply a mistake. It is a sin. To Jesus the crime of crimes is to be merely ineffectual, inept and useless. To be convinced of this it is only necessary to turn to the parables of judgment Jesus taught. Every disaster is the result, not of some wrong thing done, but of some right thing left undone. The 5 foolish bridesmaids had the door shut in their faces, not because they had become unclean, but because they had no oil (Matthew 25:10). The man of one talent was flung upon the pile of worthless things, not because he had squandered his talent, but because he had refused to invest it

> To Jesus the crime of crimes is to be merely ineffectual, inept, and useless.

(Matthew 25:30). The fig tree we are now focused on was ordered cut down, not because it was bearing fruit that was poisonous, but because it was bearing no fruit at all. The man out of whom the unclean spirit had been cast entered into a slavery sevenfold worse than the one from which he had been set free. This was the case, not because he had deliberately reached forth his hand to the unclean, but rather because his hands were empty (Luke 11:24-26). All the parables of judgment highlight the sin of uselessness.

This tree was not only useless. It was a positive hindrance. It was "in the way." As the owner asked, *"Why should it even use up the soil?"* Since it did not give an account of itself in terms of fruit, it was a parasite. It was taking to itself the sunshine and the rain. It was receiving the properties of the soil, the attention and care of the vine dresser, and giving absolutely nothing in return. To bear no fruit, therefore, is not only to be useless, but it is to be a serious obstacle to the kingdom.

How many church members live in constant neglect of their privileges and obligations? One day they stood before the altar of the church and took a solemn vow to attend its services and support its institutions. It was a vow they made, not to the pastor nor to the congregation, but to God Himself. Then they forget this high and solemn pledge. They become indifferent to the institution of which they are a part. In so doing, chances are they lose the sense of God in their lives. But even if this is not the case, by their neglect they declare to others that the church is, after all, an institution of no value. They help to lower the morale of the congregation of which they are a part. They make enthusiastic loyalty and devotion a little more difficult, and indifference and neglect a little easier for every one of their fellow members. Consenting to be useless, they become an actual hindrance.

Too often such indifference hardens into antagonism. For instance, people who persistently neglect their church have to find some excuse for so doing in order to save their own self respect and to justify themselves in the eyes of others. Therefore, many tend to become faultfinders. They begin seeking for the worst in the church instead of for the best. And seeking, they find. They then tell us with a fine show of righteous indignation that the reason they have become antagonistic to the institution to which they once pledged their loyalty is because of the evils that they enumerate. The plain truth of the matter is that they began by being useless and then degenerated into critics and faultfinders in order to justify their uselessness.

Since fruitlessness does not result in immediate destruction, some are led to believe no such results will ever follow. The fact that the penalty is not visited at once is due to the mercy of God. *"Let it alone this year also,"* pleads the vine dresser. The fact that we have been spared in spite of our uselessness does not mean this inevitable law has forgotten to operate. It only means that God is doing His loving best to bring us to our possibilities. Let us not be blinded by His very mercies, as we too often are. Jesus Himself has stepped in, giving us the second chance we desperately need. The Book of 1 John states, *"My little children, I am writing you these things so that you may not sin. But if anyone does sin, we have an advocate with the Father—Jesus Christ the righteous One"* (2:1).

Our Way of Escape

How, then, shall we escape this threefold tragedy of uselessness, of being a hindrance, and ultimate destruction? In plain words, here is the way of escape: *"Unless you repent, you will all likewise perish"* (Luke 13:5). By repentance Jesus means more than our being convicted of sin. He means more than our being sorry for sin. The repentance Jesus requires means a turning from barrenness to fruitfulness. There is more involved in this, of course, than feverish activity on our part. Certainly the first step toward usefulness is rightness with God. It is absolutely essential to be our best if we would do our best. We can all look back and evaluate our performance conscientiously, and in doing this we would have to admit there have been great periods of time when we were not very productive as fig trees in the vineyard of God. We have not brought forth the fruit that would make us properly proud or be pleasing to God.

While some missed opportunities may be irretrievable, we can rejoice in the fact that we do have the present and, if the Lord leads, some portion of the future. We each need to decide whether and how we will respond to the working of God's Spirit within our hearts and whether and how we will cooperate with the Father to be productive plants rather than barren ones. We need to be a benefit and not a hindrance to the church. We need to remember the church is more than a place. It is the body of Christ in the world today through which Christ carries on His work. In and through the church, we can serve our Lord.

> **We need to be a benefit and not a hindrance to the church.**

What can be done to reestablish the right relationship with God we all desperately need? Instead of neglecting and ignoring the Holy Spirit, let us recognize Him and respond positively. The Spirit will create within us a hunger for fellowship with God and He will lay on us the blessing of a burden of compassionate concern for those who are around us.

As missional leaders, we must recognize and confess our sin before our Lord. We must recognize that while sin may affect many lives, ultimately we have sinned against God, and it is His heart that is broken. We must plead for forgiveness and cleansing, and recognize that Jesus has enabled our forgiveness through His shed blood. We must let God recreate in us a new heart. Only God can do what needs to be done. He alone brings life, light, and love. He alone can give us spiritual heart transplants. This is all very basic Christian truth, but there is no harm in reviewing.

I encourage us to ponder the following personal inventory.

Personal Inventory

Fruits of the Spirit	Corresponding Leadership Characteristics
Love	willingness to love people regardless of status
Joy	a commitment to the task that is independent of circumstances
Peace	a commitment to an unshakable inner calling
Patience	a willingness to see beyond the horizon of trouble and obstruction a gentle spirit which is kind to those who oppose your leadership
Kindness	the kind of spirit which children see in an adult and are drawn to
Goodness	a lifestyle of integrity at every level
Faithfulness	becoming a person of absolute dependence and consistency
Gentleness	the ability to be strong at the right time and transparent at all times
Self-control	the ability to be angry at the right time and exceedingly patient at the right times

Spiritual character counts, and the type of character we need today is the character of our Lord Jesus. That character is expressed powerfully in the list of spiritual fruits. Does our missional leadership reflect these attributes? As told earlier, the story of Edward Braddock teaches us never to underestimate the Enemy, for if we do so it invites dire consequences upon our lives and those with whom we have influence. The Enemy would wish for missional leaders to focus on very worldly characteristics, but our Lord Jesus encourages us to focus on the fruitfulness God requires.

Focusing on Joy

Many things happen when we focus on the gifts of the Spirit. One of the psalms of David says *"for with You is life's fountain. In Your light we will see light"* (36:9). And Jesus said, *"But whoever drinks from the water that I will give him will never get thirsty again—ever! In fact, the water I will give him will become a well of water springing up within him for eternal life"* (John 4:14). Paul writes about the benefits of the life-giving fountain when he speaks some practical counsel to the Philippians. In the fourth chapter, he writes a description of the benefits of focusing on the gifts of the Spirit (10–23). God has an unfailing fountain of spiritual blessings awaiting the Christian who has the faith to drink from it. The fountain is the source of abundant, deep, and internal joy.

The early Christian congregation at Philippi cared for Paul, and this was the occasion for his joy in the Lord. In expressing his appreciation, the Apostle to the Gentiles used different images, including the image of a tree or a plant. It had been barren in the winter, and then it sprouted new shoots or flowers in the spring. For a long time, the Philippian Christians were barren in expressing their care for him. Now they were blossoming anew with thoughts for his welfare. He declared that their barrenness was not due to a lack of concern but a lack of opportunity. Support from Christian friends is a source of great encouragement and joy in the Lord.

Paul is making very clear that his joy at the gift from the Philippians was not because he was in dire straights at the time it arrived with himself in poverty—apparently he either did not need or did not want their money—but because he saw in this act of generosity a truly Christian deed of sacrificial, giving love. Do we have joy in the Lord in our hearts? Some Christians have been so cold so long that they would not know what this passage is talking about.

This fountain of life is the source of abiding contentment. Contentment is that gift of God that gives us serenity, frees us from worry, and enables a new sufficiency. For the Stoics, it was a state of mind where a man was entirely independent of all things—where he abolished all desires and emotions. Even love was forbidden. But Paul does not promote self-sufficiency. He believed in God-sufficiency. Paul could have nothing or everything because he learned to be content in any circumstance. This contentment is a peace coming from the knowledge that we can do all things through Christ.

> Contentment is that gift of God that gives us serenity.

Most people in our world seek contentment in accumulation. Jay Gould was a multimillionaire, yet on his deathbed, he said "I am the most miserable man in America." Commodore Vanderbilt, living in a mansion of 250 rooms on a 25,000 acre estate, owner of steamship lines and railroads, copper mines, coal mines, and thousands of acres of timber lands, said this to his physician when death drew nigh: "I am poor and needy." When dying, Alexander the Great said: "Thrust my hands through my shroud that the world may see that they're empty." The simple morale? People don't find true peace and contentment in money and material possessions.

Paul Getty lived in Sutton, England, in a magnificent mansion. He had a 700-acre estate surrounded by a great big barbed-wire iron fence with guards and vicious dogs and sirens and bells, and all the rest. But he was afraid of airplanes, afraid of crackpots, afraid of ships, afraid of old age, afraid of disease, afraid of helplessness—afraid of just about everything. Getty said, "Money can't buy anybody happiness. Just money itself can't make anybody happy."

Only Jesus Christ brings contentment. I am not speaking of being satisfied with a second-class Christianity, but being content with a first-class relationship. Missional leader, are you content?

The fountain of life is the source not only of abiding contentment, but also of adequate strength. The Apostle Paul said, *"I am able to do all things through Him who strengthens me"* (Philippians 4:13), Christ's strength was adequate for Paul when he was abased in humility, when the dark bars encircled him, when suffering came, and when death hovered nearby (2 Corinthians 4:8–12). He received strength adequate for his missionary task, and we can receive the same strength for ours, allowing us to cope with all prosperous and adverse circumstances.

Paul did not necessarily perceive in himself a strong and totally independent soul. United with Christ, however, the Source of ultimate power gave him the ability to face life forcefully. Whatever God calls us to do, He empowers us to do. The Christian call, especially of a missional leader, must be "My God is able."

God's promise is the promise of His strength. Still, many believers continue to live a powerless second-class Christianity. Many outside the Christian faith continue to reject the claims of Christ because we have failed in our Christian walk. The non-Christian rarely sees any difference in the quality and power of our daily lives. Why do we hold back? No excuse will be adequate when we stand before God. We certainly will not be able to say we held back because we lacked the strength. The reality is we do have the strength, and Christ is the source of our strength. Paul said *"Be strengthened by the Lord and by His vast strength"* (Ephesians 6:10).

Are we searching for God's unfailing fountain? Will we find it? There is abiding contentment, adequate strength, and abundant joy to be found at the fountain. We just have to come and drink, and challenge our world to do the same. There is so much to receive from our Lord. The missional leader is a person of spiritual fruitfulness who neglects not a single aspect of the unfailing fountain of God. I pray that as a missional leader, you will experience all of this as well.

Reflections

1. What does it mean that a missional leader is a person of Christlike fruitfulness?

2. What is the gift of contentment? How can we imitate Paul in being content in every circumstance?

3. Have we failed in our Christian walk to the extent that non-Christians examine us and reject the claims of Christ? How could this be possible?

CHAPTER 6

A Missional Leader
Is a Person Who Is a Team Worker

Some people are true leaders and are quite proud of themselves. Some wish to brag about their accomplishments, abilities, and accolades. Bubba was bragging to his boss one day, "You know, I know everyone there is to know. Just name someone, anyone, and I know them." Tired of his boasting, his boss called his bluff.

"All right, Bubba, how about Tom Cruise?"

"Sure, yes," said Bubba. "Tom and I are old friends, and I can prove it."

So Bubba and his boss flew out to Hollywood and knocked on Tom Cruise's door. Sure enough, Tom Cruise shouts, "Bubba! Great to see you! You and your friend come right in and join me for lunch!" Although quite impressed, Bubba's boss was still skeptical. After they leave Cruise's house he tells Bubba he thinks knowing Cruise was just lucky.

"No, no, just name anyone else," Bubba says.

"The President," his boss quickly retorts.

"Yep," Bubba says, "I know him, let's fly out to see him." And off they went. At the White House, the President spots Bubba on the tour and motions him and his boss over.

"Bubba, what a surprise. I was just on my way to a meeting, but you and your friend come on in and let's have a cup of coffee first and catch up." Well, the boss is very shaken by now, but still not totally convinced. After they leave the White House grounds, he expresses his doubts to Bubba, who again implores him to name anyone else.

"The Pope," his boss replies.

"Sure!" says Bubba. "I've known the Pope a long time." So off they flew to Rome.

Bubba and his boss are assembled with the masses in Vatican Square when Bubba says, "This will never work. I can't catch the Pope's eye among all these people. Tell you what, I know all the guards, so let me just go upstairs and I'll come out on the balcony with the Pope." And he disappeared into the crowd and headed toward St. Peter's. Sure enough, half an hour later, Bubba emerges with the Pope on the balcony. But by the time Bubba returns, he finds that his boss has had a heart attack and is surrounded by paramedics. Working his way to his boss' side, Bubba asks him, "What happened?"

> A missional leader does not believe in "using" people for a task.

His boss looks up and says, "I was doing fine until you and the Pope came out on the balcony and the Japanese tourist next to me asked, "Who's that on the balcony with Bubba?"

The next time you feel special in your own eyes, remember that Bubba knows more people than you do! Seriously, by definition, a missional leader is a person who must have a following. The missional leader is in a position to influence groups or causes for some particular task. A missional leader does not believe in "using" people for a task. A missional leader is one who believes they are part of a cause greater than themselves. They believe their team is part of a larger movement from God to accomplish His will. A missional leader does not seek to develop a following to appear to be greater or more powerful. A missional leader develops a following for the glory of the kingdom! As a part of this intentional leadership, the missional leader sees himself or herself as a part of the team. Yes, leadership is acknowledged, but the leader is simply seen as part of the process of involving others to create a true cohesive effort.

Nehemiah modeled this type of leadership as he dealt with an issue of social injustice. The current leaders had truly abused the people through unfair taxation and exorbitant economic oppression. Nehemiah's sense of justice was offended: He said in Nehemiah chapter five, *"I became extremely angry when I heard their outcry and these complaints"* (v. 6). He did not act rashly, but *"After seriously considering the matter, I accused the nobles and officials…"* (v. 7). This was not an individual effort. *"So I summoned the priests and made everyone take an oath to do this"* (v. 12b). This was a team effort for the problem was systemic and needed group action.

Remembering God and One Another

In fact, the entire Book of Nehemiah shows team spirit and the ability to work within the framework of the people of God. Nehemiah admonished the people to remember the Lord, who is great and awesome, and at the same time he admonished them to fight for their brothers and other family members (4:14). Interestingly, he also said, *"Our God will fight for us!"* (4:20). While some critics find these verses to be contradictory, the truth is that in Nehemiah's witness as to the power of the Lord, he did not neglect the need for personal and corporate responsibility. He believed God would enable the team to do His will and His work. Nehemiah exhibited a missional leadership as he drew together this body to do a powerful task. The ability to focus a group of people in a singular direction shows great vision. The implementation of a plan or strategy is extremely important, because the missional leader does not set the vision and then leave the people on their own. The missional leader is a team worker who does not wish to miss a single opportunity to strengthen the team.

Nothing is more haunting than a clear reminder of a lost opportunity that will never present itself again. To miss an opportunity like that is a sobering experience. Many missional leaders miss out on tremendous opportunities as well. Some people like to see themselves as great leaders, but at the same time they find themselves detached, separated from their people. The people whom they seek to lead simply do not want to follow them. They look back to see if others are following only to find them in the far distance. As one man teasingly said to his pastor, "Pastor, we're behind you, just way, way behind you." I am firmly convinced that a multitude of opportunities lie before us and are being missed with depressing regularity.

Decisive Faithfulness to God

Missional leaders must become people of decision, and the decisions we make now will affect others later.

The true story is told that began with a disenchanted and frustrated Seventh Day Adventist preacher. He began feeling unappreciated and misunderstood. He moved into a new type of theology and developed a core group of followers called the Branch Davidians. He changed his name from Vernon Howell to David Koresh. Among his followers were a group of men, women, and children who all formed a new cult. They barricaded themselves in a compound outside Waco, Texas. Most of you know the story. When reports of the hoarding of illegal arms, ammunition, and explosives were authenticated, the Federal agents became involved in what became a horrible situation, one that led to the death of all those in the compound. Among those in the group were precious children who had no idea what was going on.

Many in our country hate the United States government. They would look for any excuse to justify the violence they wish desperately to commit against the government. Some young men decided to do just that and developed a bomb out of fertilizer and fuel oil. They placed it in a truck parked in front of the Federal building in Oklahoma City. The second most horrible act of domestic terrorism in the history of the United States occurred when that bomb blew up and destroyed the Federal building. Many were killed, including small children. Some decisions are monumental and affect many. Others are small and may involve only ourselves. Most of the time, however, we are not thinking about where our decisions may lead. The missional leader recognizes that decisions will have an impact on the entire team and the larger evangelical movement.

Joshua 24:14–18 tells of a powerful time in the life of one missional leader who was a person of decision.

> *"Therefore, fear the LORD and worship Him in sincerity and truth. Get rid of the gods your ancestors worshiped beyond the Euphrates River and in Egypt, and worship the LORD. But if it doesn't please you to worship the LORD, choose for yourselves today the one you will worship: the gods your fathers worshiped beyond the Euphrates River, or the gods of the Amorites in whose land you are living. As for me and my family, we will worship the LORD."*

The people replied, "We will certainly not abandon the LORD to worship other gods! For the LORD our God brought us and our fathers out of the land of Egypt, the place of slavery and performed these great signs before our eyes. He also protected us all along the way we went and among all the peoples whose lands we traveled through. The LORD drove out before us all the peoples, including the Amorites who lived in the land. We too will worship the LORD, because He is our God."
—Joshua 24:14–18

Joshua was nearing the end of his life. The Bible contains the record of his farewell address and his challenge to the tribes of Israel. The future blessing of the entire nation of Israel depended on whether they would listen to their beloved leader. Above all, Joshua did not want Israel to forget or forsake their heritage. His words were massively important for God's people, and that is as true today as it was then. He helps us clear the smokescreen of life so we can clearly see the basic issues and choices open before us, and He helps us make the right decision.

The Israelites realized it was God Almighty who had rescued them in miraculous ways from Egypt. God loved them. Even when they rebelled with a stiff-necked pride, God continued to love them. He saved them from all their enemies, helping them defeat not only the Egyptians, but the Amorites, and the Amalekites. Joshua recites the gracious acts of God in Israel's behalf from patriarchal times until the occupation of Canaan. Not only had He saved them from their enemies, He had also sustained them. Even in the roughest desert, God provided all the water they needed, and manna and quail from heaven.

God alone can meet the real needs of our lives. We need to recognize His all important place. It is God who brought us here, who has given us life, who sustains and guides us each day.

God is our refuge and strength,
a helper who is always found
in times of trouble.
Therefore we will not be afraid,
though the earth trembles
and the mountains topple
into the depths of the seas,
though its waters roar and foam
and the mountains quake with its turmoil.
The LORD of Hosts is with us;
the God of Jacob is our stronghold.
—Psalm 46:1–3, 11

God alone claims our allegiance, and we are admonished to fulfill our covenant obligations. The Israelites had a problem in that their allegiance was somewhat inconsistent. Even after seeing God at work, they continued to hold on to the old gods from Egypt. They also had a practice of mixing the worship of the true God with idolatrous elements from heathen religions. Perhaps they were not as guilty in their mixed allegiance as their forefathers, but still they failed to totally commit themselves to the Lord.

Joshua commanded the people to put away all other allegiances and serve the Lord. They were commanded to serve Him in sincerity and in truth. This means that possibly for the first time, they were to serve God without hypocrisy, in simplicity, and with the truth of a committed heart. Their allegiance was found not in words of promise, but in a service to God. Israel was called to a new level of faithfulness in fulfilling the covenant. It is the same level of faithfulness to which we are called.

A pastor was asked to define faithful attendance, and he replied, "All I ask is that we apply the same standards of faithfulness to our church that we would apply to other areas of life. If your car starts one time out of three tries, do you consider it faithful? If the paper boy skips Monday and Thursday editions, is he being faithful? If you fail to come to work two or three times a month, would your boss call you faithful? If your refrigerator quits for a day now and then, do you excuse it and say, "Oh, it works most of the time!" If your hot water nozzle greets you one or two days a week with cold water, would it be faithful? If you missed two mortgage payments in a year's time, would your mortgage holder be happy and say, "Oh well, 10 out of 12 payments isn't bad?" If you made it on time to football, basketball or band practice only one in four practices, would you start the game or be a member of the band?"

> **Israel was called to a new level of faithfulness in fulfilling the covenant.**

The one thing required of a servant is that he be faithful to his master. We, too, must put away our gods. We must cease mixing our allegiance to God with other motives and purposes in our daily lives. Rather than making grand statements of faithfulness and love, the missional leader must show his or her faithfulness by living for Him. This is not to be done out of guilt or habit, but out of love for the Master.

We are admonished to declare publicly our loyalty to the Master. Joshua led Israel in a public declaration of obedience to the Lord. The Jewish people declared they would not forsake the Lord. Then Joshua set up a stone for the people to remember their declaration. Nothing helps God's people any more than to show the seriousness of their commitment by a public declaration. In today's world, a public declaration of loyalty to the Lord can be given with a spoken testimony, a baptism, evangelism, teaching, the Lord's Supper, and in hundreds of other ways.

Joshua lays it all down when he says, *"Choose for yourselves today the one you will worship."* Choose for yourselves today the one you will serve is an all-important decision. If we are going to be missional leaders, we have to draw a line in the sand and take a side by making a commitment. Yes, it will affect us and others very dramatically, but a choice must be made. Joshua made his decision by stating, *"As for me and my family, we will worship the LORD"* (Joshua 1:8). The missional leader needs to make the same decision and model the right kind of spirit.

Partnering in the Gospel

In the New Testament, the Apostle Paul exhibited this kind of spirit when he said in Philippians 1:3–5, *"I give thanks to my God for every remembrance of you, always praying with joy for all of you in my every prayer, because of your partnership in the gospel from the first day until now."* Paul spoke of the partnership in the gospel that he had with the dear people in the church at Philippi. Missional leaders will always recognize the need to be partners with the people of God, and to work alongside them in spreading the gospel.

I praise the Lord that, over the years, churches I've served all saw dramatic increases in mission involvement. I have tried to encourage this involvement through a personal partnership. In fact, as a young pastor I began going on mission trips. I had heard the teasing stories about how preachers did not like to work, so I made a promise to myself in those early days that no person would outwork me on any trip. I set out to show that I was a part of the team and would work as hard or harder than anyone else. Fortunately, to date, I have been able to make that promise come true. I continue to go on mission trips with our people. Just a couple of years ago I stayed in a tent an entire week in Mozambique as we did a church-planting project. I have traveled in dugout canoes in jungle rivers and walked desert trails in Africa. I have worked among the *favelas* or slums of Brazil, as well as survived the extremely cold winter of the Ukraine—all while working alongside God's people.

God never calls missional leaders to be lone wolves. If we are going to be leaders of spiritual fruitfulness, we are to be team workers. In the Old Testament Book of Numbers (13:17–33), we see the people of God, weary of wandering, send 12 spies into the Promised Land. They were sent from the desert area of the south to the north of the land of Canaan. Their instructions primarily were to bring reports about the land and the way it was built up and cultivated. As a part of the report, they were to find out whether the inhabitants were strong and numerous, or rather weak and few. The scouts went from Kadesh in the wilderness of Paran and on to Rehob, near the entrance of Hamath at the northernmost boundary of Canaan near Dan. The report of the land was a glowing one. The fruit they brought back was luscious, as it came from the valley of Eshcol, which was famous as a grape producing area. (The word itself means *cluster*.) The land flowed with milk and honey, the foods and goods to make a land most desirable in the eyes of the people who had been traveling in the wilderness so many years.

The two spies bringing back an encouraging and positive report had a difficult time. While all the others who went into the Promised Land recognized the land was worth taking, only Joshua and Caleb expressed their belief in the possibility that

> God never calls missional leaders to be lone wolves.

the land could be taken successfully by the people of God. The others all spoke of the ferocity of the Anakites and Nephilim, inhabitants so big the Jews stood no chance taking possession of the land. Ten out of 12 scouts balked at the mission. They even exaggerated somewhat in their report! *"To ourselves we seemed like grasshoppers, and we must have seemed the same to them"* was how the ten spies lied (Numbers 13:33*b*).

How is this related to missional leadership? That is expressed by Caleb in verse 30 of the text. *"Then Caleb quieted the people in the presence of Moses and said, 'We must go up and take possession of the land because we can certainly conquer it!'"* God blessed the kind of spirit Caleb exhibited.

> *None of these men in this evil generation will see the good land I swore to give your fathers, except Caleb the son of Jephunneh. He will see it, and I will give him and his descendants the land on which he has set foot, because he followed the Lord completely.*
> —Deuteronomy 1:35–36

Caleb had a big vision, and an undisputable sense of call. At the same time, he was a team worker. He did not have a lone ranger perspective. He did not say this was something a small group could do. His confidence was in the larger team. He could see God's hand lead them to victory together. That's how missional leaders work.

Reflections

1. The Book of Nehemiah shows team spirit and the ability to work within a framework of the people of God. How did Nehemiah model missional leadership?

2. What opportunities have you missed due to indecision?

3. What is the one thing required of a servant to his master?

4. I believe God never calls missional leaders to be lone wolves. Do you agree with this? Why or why not?

CHAPTER 7

A Missional Leader
Is a Person of Prayer

In *A Prophet with Honor*, author William Martin writes,

"In a desperate attempt to break free of the miasmic [condition] produced by the depression, with its merciless mortgage foreclosures, ruinous bank failures, and debilitating disappearance of businesses and jobs, a group of 30 or so members of the Charlotte Christian Men's Club…formed in the aftermath of Billy Sunday's 1924 revival, met in a grove of trees in Frank Graham's pasture for a daylong session of prayer and fasting…. Standing, sitting or kneeing on blankets, the men importuned God for some insight, some direction, some inspiration that would enable them to endure the doldrums in which they were adrift. They girded themselves for an evangelistic effort they hoped would generate some wave of vitality in what they regarded as Charlotte's moribund spiritual life.

The percentage of churchgoing folk in Charlotte was reportedly the highest in the nation, but these men felt the churches had become self-satisfied and smug, with little real concern for lost souls. As the intensity and confidence of their prayers began to mount, they called on God to use them 'to shake up the whole state of North Carolina for Christ.' Before long they had expanded their horizons to include the entire world. No transcript of this session exists, but one shining arrow fired toward heaven in a moment of high aspiration has been recovered…

At some point, Vernon Patterson, the group's leader, launched what must have seemed an improbable entreaty when he earnestly prayed that 'out of Charlotte the Lord would raise up someone to preach the gospel to the ends of the earth.' Surely, none of the modest group gathered there among the pines considered for a moment that the evangelist envisioned in that long-shot request was pitching hay into feed troughs a few hundred yards away, and no one would have been more surprised than he. When a friend who had come home with him after school asked why all the cars were there, Billy [Graham] told him, 'Oh, I guess they are just some fanatics who talked Dad into letting them use the place.'"

Think of the incredible results from one humble prayer group! The Book of Nehemiah yields many clues behind Nehemiah's success as a leader. Indeed, he was a missional leader par excellence. His leadership was more than singularly focused; it encompassed a number of areas. The issue before us at this point—prayer—is one that cannot be overestimated. Its power and importance in Nehemiah's life was evident, just as it must be for any person wishing to be a godly leader. When King Artaxerxes inquired as to Nehemiah's desires, Nehemiah's first response was to go to the Lord in prayer before he dared answer the king. He was a person of prayer who prayed at all times, especially in times of distress.

Listen, our God, for we are despised. Make their insults return on their own heads and let them be taken as plunder to a land of captivity.
—Nehemiah 4:4

So we prayed to our God and stationed a guard because of them day and night.
—Nehemiah 4:9

Remember me favorably, my God, for all that I have done for this people.
—Nehemiah 5:19

My God, remember Tobiah and Sanballat for what they have done, and also Noadiah the prophetess and the other prophets who wanted to intimidate me.
—Nehemiah 6:14

Remember me for this, my God, and don't erase the good deeds I have done for the house of my God and for its services.
—Nehemiah 13:14

Remember them, my God, for defiling the priesthood as well as the covenant of the priesthood and the Levites.
—Nehemiah 13:29

Nehemiah prayed that the Father would remember him with favor. As believers, we know God will never forget or forsake us.

But there are times when our hearts cry out to the Lord for His recognition and affirmation. It was so in the life of Nehemiah, and remember, he was a true prayer warrior!

Many wonder if they can ever be great leaders. Some believe one must have a specific personality type in order to lead with great effectiveness. While I admit missional leadership may be easier for some than others, I believe the principle of prayer can make great leaders of any personality type.

> The principle of prayer can make great leaders of any personality type.

Where does a leader receive his or her calling? Is it not in prayer where God speaks to most of us, revealing a calling to service and submission? Is it not in prayer that most leaders receive a vision and purpose from the Lord? Don't most missional leaders experience a heightening of burden and concern during prayer? Is it not in prayer when we become more Christlike in our spirit? Is it not in prayer where we receive a deepening concern for other team members?

Prayer provides power

Prayer is, of course, important for any believer, but for the missional leader, it is essential, not optional. Nehemiah's example is profound; yet look at other great men and women throughout Scripture to see their lives of prayer. They were in touch with a Holy God and through prayer they received the kind of strength and direction only He could give. Think about the great leaders in Scripture and their commitment to prayer as a way to discern the will of God and to receive strength to follow that will.

Moses's prayer life is described this way: *"The LORD spoke with Moses face to face, just as a man speaks with his friend"*

(Exodus 33:11). Is it any wonder Moses was the leader able to take the Hebrews from Egypt to Israel?

Who could question the leadership of King David? The prayer life of David was one of great intimacy with the Lord. In one of the most difficult times of his life, his reaction shows that prayer was of extreme importance to him. In 1 Samuel (30:6), at a time of great personal angst, his own troops talked about stoning him. In the face of this, the Bible says, *"David found strength in the LORD His God."* Psalm 51 shows another time when David went before the Lord in personal repentance, contrition, and submission. His prayer life is one for all missional leaders to follow.

Other leaders displayed this same kind of commitment to prayer. King Hezekiah went to the Lord at a point of personal need and, *"prayed to the LORD and He spoke to him and gave him a miraculous sign"* (2 Chronicles 32:24). There could be no greater prayer experience than that which the prophet Isaiah reported when he *"saw the LORD seated on a high and lofty throne"* (Isaiah 6:1). What a connection he experienced with the Lord that day! The book of Jeremiah is like an ongoing prayer dialogue between the prophet Jeremiah and the Lord. The phrase found in Jeremiah 7:1 is indicative of many throughout the book where, *"the word that came to Jeremiah from the LORD…"* A similar pattern is found with Ezekiel as in Ezekiel 30:1, *"The word of the LORD came to me…"*

The prayer life of Daniel holds promise for us all. The Bible says that *"three times a day he got down on his knees, prayed, and gave thanks to his God"* (Daniel 6:10). No matter what circumstance, this prayer warrior would not be dissuaded from his prayer practice. He knew where the power came from. Even the pouting prophet Jonah knew where his source of strength was. Jonah 2:1 shows the beginning of a wonderful time of prayer for Jonah, even though it was in the belly of a great fish!

The New Testament also reveals the tremendous prayer life on which God's great men and women depended. The Gospel of Luke shows the ongoing prayer relationship of Mary with the Lord. She asks the angel why she had been chosen for such a grand task (1:34). Her pure heart was open to the Lord. *"'I am the Lord's slave,' said Mary. 'May it be done to me according to your word'"* (1:38) Another example is that of the Apostle Paul, who displayed a prayer life of power and passion. Acts 16:25 shows him to be much in the habit of prayer, even at midnight. Ephesians 1:16 is among the many verses showing the prayer life of the apostle. *"I never stop giving thanks for you as I remember you in my prayers."*

Obviously, the greatest prayer leader of all is our Lord Jesus. There can be no greater prayer ever prayed than the one recorded in the seventeenth chapter of the Gospel of John. In that great chapter, often called The High Priestly Prayer, Jesus prays as God the Son to God the Father. He prays for Himself in verses one through five, and He prays for all the disciples in verses six through nineteen. Then the Lord prays for all believers (17: 20–26). Be encouraged, you are on the prayer list of Jesus!

Prayer Praxis in Action

There is no missional leadership without a serious commitment to prayer. No one would argue that there are many great leaders in this world who do not pray. But there are no great *missional* leaders who do not pray.

Nehemiah's prayer life was one where action followed prayer. Nehemiah writes, *"So we prayed to our God and stationed a guard because of them day and night"* (4:9). In other words, Nehemiah exhibits powerful prayer, but also powerful action. Missional leaders need to be willing to spend time in prayer but also to apply the principles of prayer in life. We must do what God has called us to do to accomplish His work.

Action must follow prayer. We are involved as believers in the reality called spiritual warfare. Spiritual warfare is overlooked by many, much to the harm of the Christian church. The Bible teaches that there is a deceptive, dangerous spirit world that distorts reality and ruins human lives. It is real, and we must not dismiss it.

A preacher was speaking about Satan and his use of demonic forces. He was also speaking about the current condition of many churches, bemoaning the fact that in many churches today, the Spirit of God no longer seems to be present. There seems to be a general lethargy that chokes spiritual life. He stated (accurately or not) that Satan has so long ago won the battle for most churches that he no longer bothers with them anymore. He said that since most churches are no longer any threat to Satan's kingdom, all he had to do was station some second-rate demon on the steeple of each church, with these instructions: "While I don't expect anything to happen, if the church ever begins to wake up, you let me know."

That scenario may not be very accurate, but it certainly makes the point that many churches, families, and individuals have surrendered to spiritual lethargy. For some, there is little chance of awakening to life. We need to expose the Enemy so we may live victoriously to fight again. I am not in this for a truce, a stalemate, and certainly not defeat.

I am praying for missional leaders and churches who will be on fire for Jesus Christ. I am praying for missional leaders and churches to see victory over dark spiritual forces, because if we lose the battle on this level, we will suffer great loss.

Sooner or later every serious believer discovers the Christian life is a battleground, and that we face an Enemy who is much stronger than we are—apart from Christ. The Apostle Paul used many military illustrations when referring to the believer's conflict with Satan. In fact, military illustrations were favorites with Paul. While he wrote the letter to the Ephesians, he himself was *"an ambassador in chains,"* bound to a Roman soldier (Ephesians 6:20). Paul's readers were certainly familiar with soldiers and the equipment they used when he wrote the following challenge:

> *Finally, be strengthened by the Lord and by His vast strength. Put on the full armor of God so that you can stand against the tactics of the Devil. For our battle is not against flesh and blood, but against the rulers, against the authorities, against the world powers of this darkness, against the spiritual forces of evil in the heavens. This is why you must take up the full armor of God, so that you may be able to resist in the evil day, and having prepared everything, to take your stand.*
> —Ephesians 6:10–13

Missional leaders of prayer know that Christians face three enemies: the world, the flesh, and the devil (Ephesians 2:1–3).

> **We face an Enemy who is much stronger than we are apart from Christ.**

The world is society without God. It is the system around us opposed to God, catering to *"the lust of the flesh, the lust of the eyes, and the pride in one's lifestyle"* (1 John 2:15–17). The flesh is the old sin nature we inherited from Adam, a nature opposed to God that can do nothing spiritual to please God. By His death and resurrection, Christ conquered the world (John 16:33; Galatians 6:14), overcame the flesh (Romans 6:1–6; Galatians 2:20), and defeated the devil (Ephesians 1:19–23). The way to see this is that, as believers, we do not fight for victory—we fight from victory! The Spirit of God enables us, by faith, to appropriate Christ's victory for ourselves.

In the closing verses of the letter to the Ephesians, Paul discussed several topics his readers would need to understand and apply in order to walk in victory. Unless we know who the Enemy is, where he is, and what he can do, we will have a difficult time defeating him. All over the Bible God instructs us about the Enemy, so there is no reason for us to be caught off guard.

Countering the Enemy

We need to identify the leader—the devil. The Enemy has many different names. The name *devil* means "accuser," because he accuses God's people day and night before the throne of God (Revelation 12:7–11). *Satan* itself means "adversary," because he is the enemy of God. He is also called the tempter (Matthew 4:3), and the murderer and the liar (John 8:44). He is compared to a roaring lion (1 Peter 5:8), a serpent and dragon (Genesis 3:1; Revelation 12:9), and an angel of light (2 Corinthians 11:13–15). He is also known as *"the god of this age"* (2 Corinthians 4:4). How does he accomplish so much? He is the leader of a band of organized helpers.

Paul called Satan's helpers *"rulers . . . authorities . . .powers of this darkness. . . spiritual forces of evil in the heavens"* (Ephesians 6:12). Charles B. Williams translates Ephesians 6:12 this way: *"For our contest is not with human foes alone, but with the rulers, authorities, and cosmic powers of this dark world; that is, with the spirit forces of evil challenging us in the heavenly contest."* This suggests a definite army of demonic creatures assists Satan in his attacks against Christian believers. The Apostle John hints that one third of the angels fell with Satan when he rebelled against God (Revelation 12:4), and Daniel wrote that Satan's angels struggle against God's angels for control of the affairs of nations (Daniel 10:13–20). A spiritual battle is going on in this world, and in the sphere of the heavenlies, and you and I are a part of this battle. Knowing this makes walking in victory a vitally important thing for all missional leaders.

Missional leaders must recognize that our battle is not against human beings but, rather, against Satan and his spiritual powers. 2 Corinthians 11:14–15 reads, *"For Satan himself is disguised as an angel of light. So it is no great thing if his servants also disguise themselves as servants of righteousness."* We are wasting our time fighting people when we ought to be fighting the devil who seeks control of people to make them oppose the work of God.

Not every wrong human action or thought is directed by some kind of demonic entity. To believe otherwise is to ascribe every action to the devil, and thus to remove ourselves from personal responsibility. Some think we are unwitting pawns at the mercy of some kind of cosmic wrestling match. The truth is, the Evil One is fully capable of taking anything in your life or mind, and using every thought, action, and situation for his glory.

> The devil seeks control of people to make them oppose the work of God.

He is the master of manipulating relationships and situations to cause division among the body of Christ, stunted growth among believers, and misunderstanding among the lost. While we spend a great deal of energy and effort trying to achieve spiritual victory in life, we can fail miserably when fighting the wrong enemies and looking in the wrong place to do battle.

Missional leaders recognize Satan's abilities. Satan is a strong enemy (Ephesians 6:10–12), and we need the power of God to stand against him. We must never underestimate the power of the devil. He is not compared to a roaring lion and a great dragon for nothing. The Book of Job gives a painful overview of what Satan's power can do to destroy a man's body, home, wealth, and friends. Jesus calls Satan a thief who comes *"to steal and to kill and to destroy"* (John 10:10). Not only is Satan tenacious, he is also wise and subtle, and we fight against *"the tactics of the devil"* (Ephesians 6:11). He is cunning and crafty.

> It all comes down to a choice between the way of God or the way of Satan.

No Christian—especially not a missional leader—can afford to be *"ignorant of his intentions"* (2 Corinthians 2:11). Some people are cunning and crafty, too, *"with cleverness in the techniques of deceit"* (Ephesians 4:14). But behind all of it is Satan, the arch-deceiver, masquerading as an angel of light (2 Corinthians 11:14) and seeking to blind people's minds to the truth of God's Word. This is a struggle, and we are not spectators at a game—we are involved in hand-to-hand combat. Satan wants to use our external enemy, the world, and our internal enemy, the flesh, to defeat us. His weapons and battle plans are formidable.

We have the victory

We need to see the way to victory. Since we are fighting against enemies in the spirit world, we need special equipment both for offense and defense. God has provided all the armor we need, and we dare not omit any part. The importance of clothing ourselves with the spiritual armor of God is so we can achieve more than a stalemate—so we can move on to victory! Paul commanded his readers to put on the armor, take the weapons, and withstand Satan, all of which we do by faith. Knowing that Christ has already conquered Satan, and knowing that spiritual armor and weapons are available, by faith we accept what God gives us and go out to meet the foe. Be strengthened by the Lord and by His vast strength because He alone is the source we need to win the victory.

The missional leader knows it all comes down to a choice between the way of God or the way of Satan. We need enlist in the army on whose side we will fight. Will we allow the demon on the steeple to rest or to flee with fright? There is an illustration that speaks to the point of this issue. An elderly Native American who had received the Lord was asked by his missionary friend how he was doing in the Christian life. He stated that there were two dogs fighting inside him. With a puzzled look, the missionary asked him what he meant. He replied that these two dogs fought constantly. One was a good dog and one was a bad dog. The missionary then asked, "Which dog is winning?"

The old Native American replied, "The one I feed the most."

Perhaps the greatest expression of God's care and provision is found in the availability of the full armor of God to help us resist the evil day and prepare to take our stand. We have to seek this spiritual armor of God on a daily basis *"for our battle is not against flesh and blood, but against the rulers, against the authorities, against the world powers of this darkness, against the spiritual forces of evil in the heavens"* (Ephesians 6:12). God calls believers to action, to responsibility, and to a spiritual preparation that takes much prayer: *"With every prayer and request, pray at all times in the Spirit and stay alert in this, with all perseverance and intercession for all the saints"* (Ephesians 6:18).

The missional leader is a person of prayer because prayer gives us a constant awareness of the spiritual battle occurring around us. Prayer gives us that uneasy feeling we have in our relationship to this world, for in the pilgrimage of the believer, and especially the missional leader, there must be an increasing separation from this world and its mind-set. Many have observed what I think is a horrible situation in modern Christianity: that we feel so at ease in this R-rated world. Rather than drawing comfort from and desiring to conform to the world, we should experience revulsion at this state of affairs. We have a warning from God on loving the world:

> *Do not love the world or the things that belong to the world. If anyone loves the world, love for the Father is not in him. Because everything that belongs to the world—the lust of the flesh, the lust of the eyes, and the pride in one's lifestyle—is not from the Father, but is from the world. And the world with its lust is passing away, but the one who does God's will remains forever.*
> —1 John 2:15–17

The New Testament word for *world* has at least three different meanings. Sometimes it means the physical world, the earth: *"God who made the world* [our planet] *and everything in it"* (Acts 17:24). Christians ought to appreciate the beauty and usefulness of the earth God has made, since He *"richly provides us with all things to enjoy"* (1 Timothy 6:17). The word also means the human world, *humankind*: *"For God loved the world in this way: He gave His One and Only Son"* (John 3:16). Sometimes these two ideas appear together: *"He* [Jesus] *was in the world, and the world* [earth] *was created through Him, yet the world* [mankind] *did not recognize Him"* (John 1:10).

But the warning *"do not love the world!"* is not about the world of nature or the world of persons. *World* in the context of this discussion refers to the invisible spiritual system opposed to God and Christ. In the Bible, the world is Satan's system for opposing the work of Christ on earth. The devil has an organization of evil spirits (Ephesians 6:11–12) working with him and influencing the affairs of "this world." The work of the devil and his cohorts is the very opposite of what is godly, holy, and spiritual, and *the whole world is under the sway of the evil one"* (1 John 5:19). Jesus called Satan *"the ruler of this world"* (John 12:31).

Just as the Holy Spirit uses Christians to accomplish God's will on earth, so Satan uses people to fulfill his evil purposes. Those who do not know Christ are dead in their sins, and whether they realize it or not, they are energized by the *"ruler of the atmospheric domain, the spirit now working in the disobedient"* (Ephesians 2:1–2).

Jesus calls these people *"the sons of this age"* (Luke 16:8). A Christian is a member of the human world, and lives in the physical world, but the believer does not belong to the spiritual world that is Satan's system for opposing God. The Gospel of John says, *"If you were of the world* [Satan's system], *the world would love you as its own. However, because you are not of the world, but I have chosen you out of it, the world hates you"* (John 15:19). This means that the world we're living in is not a natural habitat for Christ followers who know their citizenship is in heaven (Philippians 3:20). All our effective resources for living on earth come from the Father in heaven.

Were it not for the Holy Spirit's living within us, and the spiritual resources we have in prayer, Christian fellowship, and the Word of God, we could never survive here on earth with any faith intact. We complain about the pollution of Earth's atmosphere, yet the atmosphere of the world that is the invisible demonic system is also so polluted spiritually that Christians cannot breathe normally!

There is a second reason Christians must not love the world. We mustn't love the world because of the world's influence.

First John says, *"Do not love the world or the things that belong to the world. If anyone loves the world, love for the Father is not in him"* (2:15). Worldliness is not so much a matter of activity as of attitude. Thus, it is possible for a Christian to stay away from disreputable, worldly temptations, and still love the world. Worldliness is a matter of the heart. To the extent that a Christian loves the world system and the things in it, he or she does not love the Father.

Worldliness not only affects one's response to the love of God, it also affects one's response to the will of God. *"And the world with its lust is passing away, but the one who does God's will remains forever"* (1 John 2:17). Doing the will of God is a joy for those living in the love of God. If we love the Lord, we will obey what He commands, but when a believer loses enjoyment of the Father's love, it hard to obey the Father's will.

These two factors taken together give a practical definition of worldliness—anything in our Christian life causing us to lose enjoyment of the Father's love or causing us to lose the desire to do the Father's will is worldly and must be avoided. One's responses to the Father's love (our personal devotional life) and to doing the Father's will (our daily conduct) are the two tests of worldliness.

Surely all things were created by God (John 1:3). How is it then that everything in the world is opposed to God and said not to originate from Him? Is everything in the world so tainted that the believer is not to desire it? The answer becomes clear when we consider the kind of specific things John has in mind. These things indicate that John is thinking of the world insofar as it has become fallen and rebellious, the source of desires that stand in opposition to the love of God.

Many things in this world are identified as wrong in the Bible. For example, it is wrong to lie and steal (Ephesians

4:25, 28), and sexual sins are wrong (Ephesians 5:1–3). About these things and many others Christians can have little or no debate. But there are areas of Christian belief and conduct that are not quite so clear and about which even the best Christian thinkers disagree.

The Apostle John warns us that the world system uses three devices to trap Christians: *"the lust* [desire] *of the flesh, the lust of the eyes, and the pride of life"* (1 John 2:16 KJV) or *"the pride in one's lifestyle."* These were the same temptations that trapped Eve and resulted in the Fall back in the Garden of Eden: *"Then the woman saw that the tree was good for food and delightful to look at, and that it was desirable for obtaining wisdom. So she took some of its fruit and ate it; she also gave some to her husband, who was with her, and he ate it"* (Genesis 3:6).

The lust or desire of the flesh is the first device. It includes anything appealing to our fallen nature. "The flesh" does not mean "the body." Rather, it refers to the basic nature of unregenerate people, making them blind to spiritual truth (1 Corinthians 2:14). Flesh is the nature we receive in our physical birth, while spirit is the nature we receive in the second, spiritual birth (John 3:5–6). A Christian has both the old nature (flesh) and the new nature (Spirit) to contend with in life. And what a battle these two natures can wage! (Galatians 5:17–23).

God has given us certain desires, and these desires are good. Hunger, thirst, and sex are good desires, and not at all evil in themselves. There is nothing wrong with eating, drinking, sleeping, or begetting children. But when the flesh nature controls them, then they become sinful "lusts." And this is how the world operates. It appeals to the normal human appetites and tempts us to satisfy them in forbidden ways. We are surrounded by a myriad of temptations and allurements appealing to our lower nature and more ignoble instincts. *"Stay*

The Nehemiah Factor

awake and pray, so that you won't enter into temptation. The spirit is willing, but the flesh is weak" (Matthew 26:41).

It is important for believers to remember that everything God says about the old nature, the flesh, is negative. In the flesh there is no good thing. *"For I know that nothing good lives in me, that is, in my flesh. For the desire to do what is good is with me, but there is no ability to do it"* (Romans 7:18). The flesh profits nothing. *"The Spirit is the One who gives life. The flesh doesn't help at all. The words that I have spoken to you are spirit and are life"* (John 6:63). Christians are not to put any confidence in the flesh (Philippians 3:3), or to make any provision for the flesh (Romans 13:14). A person who lives for the flesh is living a negative life.

The second device the world uses to trap the Christian is the lust of the eyes. We sometimes forget that the eyes have an appetite. Have you ever heard the phrase, "Feast your eyes on this"? The lust of the flesh appeals to the lower appetites of the old nature, tempting us to indulge them in sinful ways. The lust of the eyes, however, operates in a more refined way. In view here are pleasures that gratify the sight and the mind—more sophisticated and intellectual pleasures. In the time of the Apostle John, the Greeks and Romans lived for entertainments and activities that excited the eyes. Times have not changed very much, in view of television and so on. Every Christian's prayer ought to be, *"Turn my eyes from looking at what is worthless"* (Psalm 119:37).

The third device is the boastful pride of life. God's glory is rich and full, but ours is vain and empty. In fact, the Greek word for "pride" was used to describe a braggart who was trying to impress people with his importance. People have always tried to outdo others in their spending and their getting. The boastful pride of life motivates much of what such people do. Why is it so many Americans buy houses, cars, appliances, and wardrobes they really cannot afford? Why do so many succumb to the "travel now, pay later" philosophy and get themselves into hopeless debt taking vacations far beyond their means? There are so many in this deplorable situation largely because they want to impress other people—because of their "pride of life." Most of us do not go that far, but it is amazing the things people do just to make an impression. Many people will even sacrifice their honesty and integrity in order to feel important.

The world appeals to Christians through the lust of the flesh, the lust of the eyes, and the pride of life. And once the world takes over in one of these areas, a Christian will gradually begin to lose enjoyment of the Father's love and his or her desire to do God's will. The Bible will become boring, and prayer a difficult chore. Even Christian fellowship may seem empty and disappointing. No one becomes worldly all of a sudden. It is a gradual process that creeps up on us. First is the friendship of the world. But James says friendship with the world is hostility toward God (James 4:4). By nature, John writes, the world and the Christian are enemies, so we shouldn't be surprised if the world hates us (1 John 3:13). It comes down to this: A Christian who is a friend of the world is an enemy of God.

The world in which we live is not permanent. The only sure thing about this world system is that it's not going to be here forever. One day the system will be gone, along with all its various attractions. It is passing away, and will not last. Only what is part of the will of God will last. Missional leaders keep themselves "loosely attached" to this world because they live for something far better. They are *foreigners and temporary residents on the earth"* (Hebrews 11:13).

In the First Letter of John, the apostle contrasts two ways of life: a life lived for eternity and a life lived for time (2:17). A worldly person lives for the pleasures of the flesh, but a dedicated Christian lives for the joys of the Spirit. A worldly person lives for what he can see, the lust of the eyes; but a spiritual believer lives for the unseen realities of God (2 Corinthians 4:8–18). A worldly person lives for the pride of life, the vainglory that appeals to mankind, but a Christian who does the will of God lives for God's approval. Slowly but inevitably, and perhaps sooner than even Christians think, the world is passing away. But the man who does God's will abides forever.

The world gets into a Christian through the heart. The missional leader recognizes the reality of spiritual warfare. He or she recognizes the Evil One is seeking to destroy everything good, pure, and holy. The adversary wishes to divert our energies and steal our passion for the Lord. It is extremely important that we follow the example of Nehemiah, the Apostle Paul, Mary, but most of all our Lord Jesus in becoming a person of serious prayer whose faith is put into action.

As a young boy I was first given a Bible by my parents on Christmas Eve 1964. It was a black King James Version Bible, and I have that Bible to this day. I believe my parents were able to afford it because it had been returned to the store. In fact, it had another boy's name embossed on the front cover. Though I tried to darken it out as best I could, that boy's name is visible to this very day. I began reading the Word of God as a young boy and began to seek His face in prayer. Spending that time with the Lord every day is not something that I see as optional. Through the years, my prayertime has been that which I credit for the Lord's great blessing upon my life. He has been so good to me! I cannot imagine going a day without spending time seeking His will from the Word and seeking His presence in prayer.

Over the years, we have developed a prayer ministry in our church that we named God's 3000. It is an attempt to involve at least 3,000 persons in some kind of intercessory prayer ministry. It is my belief that this prayer ministry, which takes many forms, is that which has given our church its great success. While we have far to go, it is my contention that the undergirding of prayer by God's people is what leads a church to greatness.

In my own life, I can truly say it is the prayers of many people across our nation that have enabled me to function at the level I have. One former denominational president told me that the day I cease to be president of the Convention, I would physically feel the prayer covering move to the next person. I thanked him for the warning, but told him I would "enjoy it while I could." Prayers from God's people unleash a reservoir of blessings upon the prayer focus that is difficult to describe. Prayer is a mystery, but its efficacious benefit is profoundly experienced by those who are the recipients.

Reflections

1. Describe the basic principles of prayer. Can prayer make great leaders out of any personality type?

2. Moses, David, Hezekiah, Daniel, and Mary all displayed a serious commitment to prayer. What was the key to their success as prayer warriors?

3. What does the author mean by saying we are fighting enemies in the spirit world? What are our weapons against them?

CHAPTER 8

A Missional Leader
Is a Person of Integrity

A missional leader must be a person of integrity. The news seems to abound always with yet another political or religious leader of high standing resigning office because of allegations of sexual impropriety. Both secular and sacred publications regularly report the disappointing news of leaders—lay and clergy—who have fallen in some immoral way. Few are surprised anymore when new allegations arise.

The generational characteristics of the younger adult generation, called the Bridger generation (which basically includes people between 18 and 29 years of age), reveal they are desperately looking for authenticity among leaders. This generation has grown up seeing virtually all promises broken to them. They have seen parents and grandparents work for companies that at one time would have provided lifetime security, only to see those companies fire or lay off people years before retirement. This generation has had the promise of a stable home broken as their parents and sometimes grandparents, in increasing numbers, have divorced one another. Interestingly enough, the fastest growing segment of population now living together without the benefit of marriage is the senior adult group. The younger generation has not seen authenticity and integrity displayed in their homes, or in their schools and in society at-large, so they are looking for it in a serious way.

The Search for Consistent Integrity in Leaders

Who is not aware that *"all have sinned and fall short of the glory of God"* (Romans 3:23)? Church people are all imperfect humans trying to point the world to a perfect God. Yet, in spite of our protestations of total depravity, the world still looks for leaders with integrity. Even among people who can overlook minor failings, there is a longing to see those whose hearts and behaviors demonstrate consistency and integrity.

The missional leader must be a person of integrity. Nehemiah's integrity was a great factor in his leadership and ability. It is interesting to note that the enemies and detractors of Nehemiah's ministry could never speak about any kind of personal failing that they might use to stop the building of the wall or to report to the king. Even the false rumors his detractors tried to spread were not personal in nature at all (6:8). In fact, Nehemiah speaks about the opposition who *"was hired, so that I would be intimidated, do as he suggested, sin, and get a bad reputation, in order that they could discredit me"* (6:13). But Nehemiah's life of integrity protected him from scandal.

> Nehemiah's life of integrity protected him from scandal.

Being a missional leader of integrity gave Nehemiah the ability to speak to his people with clarity and power, and at times with a prophetic word of exhortation. He said to them, *"What you are doing isn't right. Shouldn't you walk in the fear of our God and not invite the reproach of our foreign enemies?"* (5:9). He was speaking of the social injustice occurring among the people of Jerusalem. His indignation was righteous, based on issues of integrity. Nehemiah said, *"I became extremely angry when I heard their outcry and these complaints"* (5:6). His sensitivity toward wrongdoing was heightened by his own personal integrity as he exhorted them against selling food on the Sabbath and led the people in a national confession of sin.

Several years ago, I became pastor of the First Baptist Church of Taylors, South Carolina. I heard the church was home to Cliff Barrows, the longtime music director for the Billy Graham Evangelistic Association. Having contact with Cliff was a blessing beyond words. He and his dear wife, Ann, have been a tremendous encouragement to me. Shortly after coming to Taylors, my family and I were able to have lunch and an extended time with Cliff and Ann Barrows. He told the story of how the Billy Graham team came together, and of the early days of struggle. He also told of the commitments they made to each another in the areas of accountability, integrity, and especially sexual propriety. In all the years that have gone by from then until now, there has never been even a hint of scandal or impropriety among the Graham team. Truly, this is a team that exhibits excellence in missional leadership integrity.

Justness, Mercifulness, and Humility

Earlier, we saw that a missional leader is a person of spiritual fruitfulness. There are two aspects of the fruit of the Spirit that apply to the topic of integrity. Galatians 5:22 speaks of the fruit of goodness. This spiritual fruit represents integrity and purity. It is given to us as part of the "basic equipment" of belonging to Jesus Christ. The twenty-third verse of Galatians 5 tells us of the spiritual fruit of self-control. Many people say at some point or another they wish they had the fruit of self-control. The truth is that every born-again believer has this spiritual fruit. It may not have been allowed to grow strong in many lives, yet it is present if the Spirit of God is present in a person's life. This is true of both goodness and self-control. We in the church desperately need to be like Nehemiah and even more so like our Lord Jesus, who both exhibited these two spiritual fruits in their most absolute form.

Robert White once spoke about the great compliments given in Scripture. One of those compliments was given to John the Baptist who was spoken of by Jesus when he said, *"I assure you: Among those born of women no one greater than John the Baptist has appeared"* (Matthew 11:11). What a grand statement! White points out that an even greater compliment was given when God said about David, *"I have found David the son of Jesse, a man after My heart, who will carry out all My will"* (Acts 13:22).

What kind of life should missional leaders live so God would say complimentary things about us? The answer is found in the writings of the prophet Micah. *"He has told you men what is good and what it is the LORD requires of you: Only to act justly, to love faithfulness, and to walk humbly with your God"* (6:8). We all know the story of King David's great failings, a story that reads like a modern-day newspaper account of a contemporary leader. After David committed the sin of adultery with Bathsheba, and even the murder of her husband, Uriah, the prophet Nathan was sent to the king. Nathan told a heart-clenching story about a rich man taking advantage of a poor man. He then waited for the king's response (2 Samuel 12:1–4). After hearing the story, King David was infuriated and spoke about his intention to bring justice to that situation because of the abuse of a poor, innocent person by a powerful oppressor. Nathan responded, *"You are the man!"* (2 Samuel 12:7).

The king could have executed Nathan on the spot. It was the prerogative of any Near Eastern king to have execution authority at his fingertips. But instead of exercising his right, David confessed he had sinned against the Lord. After this, he lived justly and in deep contrition. No doubt it was then that God knew David's heart was submitted to His own.

The Bible also tells us loving mercy should be part of our lifestyle of integrity. The Hebrew word for "mercy" means lovingkindness, faithfulness. David exhibited this lifestyle as well. One day, as he reflected on his boyhood days, David remembered his dear friend Jonathan. At this point, Jonathan had long since died. He wondered if anyone in Jonathan's family was alive so that he might minister to them. He was then told of Mephibosheth, a crippled young man, Jonathan's son. David called

> **What God expects has not changed across the ages.**

him to his palace and told him of his love for his father. He told him he would restore Jonathan's kingdom to him. The prophet Micah tells us a lifestyle of mercy and integrity means acting justly, loving faithfulness, and walking humbly with God (6:8). There is no question David loved mercy.

One of the finest pictures of humility is found in the fifty-first Psalm. This psalm shows David as a man of deep contrition, confession, and repentance after his rebellion with Bathsheba. He cries out, *"Be gracious to me, God, according to Your faithful love; according to Your abundant compassion, blot out my rebellion"* (51:1). This prayer of restoration reveals David had a heart like His. Even though the king could have been unrepentant and denied Nathan's charge, he did what was right and good, loving mercy, and walking humbly before God.

What God expects from us as missional leaders has not changed across the ages. What He expected thousands of years ago, He expects in the twenty-first century. He wants to give amazing compliments and offer kind words to each of us. Do our lives manifest just and right living? Can we speak with clarity and power, as Nehemiah did? Do our lives show the love of mercy? Do our hearts resonate with concern for the lost, hurting, and dying of our world? Have we so segregated ourselves within the walls of the church that we no longer understand the concern Christ had for the hurting? Are we walking humbly before the Lord? These are the marks of a life of integrity. The missional leader possesses a moral authority coming from a humble, merciful, and just style of life. This is what is good, and what the Lord requires when we deal with issues of ambition, power, careerism, and all the other concerns that seem to dominate the lives of so many Christian leaders.

Do you dream for this kind of lifestyle? Do you want to strike blows for the kingdom? Do you hope God will compliment you? Do you want a style of leadership profoundly possessing moral authority? Do not despair, do not waver in your faith, and do not give up your dreams. God is ready to help.

> *Now may the God of peace, who brought up from the dead our Lord Jesus—the great Shepherd of the sheep—with the blood of the everlasting covenant, equip you with all that is good to do His will, working in us what is pleasing in His sight, through Jesus Christ, to whom be glory forever and ever.*
> —Hebrews 13:20–21

This benediction gathers together the major themes of the Book of Hebrews: peace, the resurrected Christ, Christ's superiority, a heavenly priesthood, the blood of the covenant, spiritual perfection (maturity), and God's work in the believer. As the Good Shepherd, Jesus Christ laid down His life for the sheep (John 10:11). As the Great Shepherd, Jesus lives for the sheep in heaven today, working on our behalf. As the Chief Shepherd, He will come for the sheep at His return and give us the unfading crown of glory (1 Peter 5:4). Our Lord cares for His own in the past, present, and future. He is the same yesterday, today, and forever.

Jesus's Promise to Mature Us

Our great High Priest is our Great Shepherd. When Jesus was on earth, He worked for us by completing the great work of redemption. *"I have glorified You on the earth by completing the work You gave Me to do"* (John 17:4). Now that He is in heaven, the Savior is working within us to mature us in His will, and to bring us to a place of spiritual perfection. We will never completely reach that place until He returns, but while we are waiting, we are told to continue growing in our faith.

What is the basis for this marvelous work of growth? It is *"the blood of the everlasting covenant"* (Hebrews 13:20). This is the New Covenant (Hebrews 8:7–13) based on the sacrifice of Christ (Hebrews 10:1–18). Because this New Covenant was a part of God's eternal plan of salvation and guarantees everlasting life, it is called "the everlasting covenant." But apart from the death of Jesus Christ, we cannot be equipped to do all that is good.

What is God's goal for us? To equip us *"with all that is good to do His will, working in us what is pleasing in His sight"* (Hebrews 13:21). The term *equip* is a medical one meaning "to set a broken bone." To fishermen it meant "to mend a broken net"; to sailors it meant "to outfit a ship for a voyage"; and to soldiers it meant "to equip an army for battle." Our Savior in heaven wants to equip us for life on earth. He wants to set the "broken bones" in our lives so we might walk straight and run our life-races successfully. He wants to repair the breaks in the nets so we might catch fish and win souls. He wants to equip us for battle and outfit us so we will not be battered in the storms of life. The primary consideration is that Jesus wants to equip and mature us so the Holy Spirit can work *in* us and *through* us to do what pleases Him and accomplishes His will.

The tools God uses to mature and equip His children are the Word of God (2 Timothy 3:16–17), prayer (1 Thessalonians 3:10), and the fellowship of the local church (Ephesians 4:11–12). He also uses individual believers to equip and restore us (Galatians 6:1). Finally, He uses suffering to perfect and discipline His children (1 Peter 5:10). God wants leaders to possess a moral authority that comes from a humble, merciful, righteous, well-pleasing style of life. God's people are calling out for a different style of leadership. They are looking for leaders who are humble and kind, mature, and fully equipped and outfitted for the battle.

Who will God compliment in heaven? Do we think it will be the great Christian leaders who have strutted across the stages of our conventions and assemblies, or do we think it will be the humble servant picking up the pencils and trash around the buildings after church? We all know the answer to that question. God is looking for men and women of integrity whose lives manifest justness, a love of mercy, and a humbleness before the Lord.

Reflections

1. Describe the Bridger generation. What are so many young adults looking for in terms of church?

2. David rebelled with Bathsheba and murdered her husband, Uriah, yet God said David had a heart like His. How could this be so?

3. What tools does God use to mature and equip His children?

CHAPTER 9

A Missional Leader
Is a Person of Comprehension

There is great deal of misunderstanding in our world about what people really need, want, and expect. The missional leader must have an awareness of the environment and the culture, as well as comprehension of what is happening at the moment. For example, the second chapter of Nehemiah shows how astute he was at discerning the mood of the king and the lay of the land. It also shows a very discerning spirit, even to the point of discerning the spiritual motives of his enemies. Nehemiah decided to keep his vision and purpose quiet for the moment because others were simply not ready to hear the grand scheme God had hatched in his heart. How desperately the church needs missional leaders and people of great discernment like Nehemiah.

One of the great examples of incredible comprehension and discernment is found in the Book of Esther, which follows Nehemiah. There, Queen Esther shows an incredible discerning spirit. In the fifth chapter of Esther, we see the queen approaching the king at exactly the right time. To have approached him and been rejected was to risk death. Esther had a discerning ability to impart only that part of the issue that the king could handle at that time. The preparing of a great banquet so that at the right moment she could reveal the truth about Haman to the king was an absolute stroke of genius and prudent discernment. Call it the miracle of timing if you like, but great leaders grasp what is going on around them and they know about the larger culture in which they live.

An exemplary illustration of perception is found in the thirteenth chapter of the Book of Numbers. This is the story of Caleb, Joshua, and the other spies Moses sent to scout out the Canaan land before entering the Promised Land. Caleb's report to Moses and Aaron was based on solid knowledge. He spoke glowingly about the land because he had been there, surveyed it, and had seen its fruit. He was a man who believed that learning a situation helps bring clarity. His response was that the land was worth taking. *"We must go up and take possession of the land because we can certainly conquer it!"* (13:30). How many times do our leaders display such vision and comprehension?

> Great leaders grasp what is going on around them and they know about the larger culture in which they live.

In 1858, an expedition went out to explore what is now called the Grand Canyon. One young army officer by the name of Lieutenant Ives wrote back in his report that the land they visited was altogether valueless. He said it could be approached only from the south, and after one arrived, there was nothing to do but to leave. Lieutenant Ives wrote that his group would be, without a doubt, the last party of Whites to ever go there, and that the land would forever remain unvisited and undisturbed.

It is probably not necessary to say, but that young lieutenant lacked vision and understanding. Caleb, Esther, and Nehemiah all had the gift of comprehension. They were all willing to learn, and to have their faith in the Lord joined by a godly common sense and strategic learning.

The ministry to which God called me is most often called "transitional pastoring." The churches I have led were in need of a transition. Most were in a stagnant and sometimes declining position before I arrived. Some were in deep distress over past difficulties. Would I rather have been called to churches where everything was strong, solid, and growing? The answer to that question is obvious, but God did not call me to that kind of ministry. Each new situation required discernment as I spent time getting to know the culture of the church. I tell young ministers they need to be very careful to become aware of the power structure of the church. They need to be careful to discern between the informal and the formal power structures because sometimes there is a great difference between the two. I encourage them to spend time getting to know the people, the situation, and the culture before making any major changes.

For a missional leader, comprehension or discernment is extremely important. Many Christians, including Christian leaders, find themselves in a state of arrested development. The Bible talks about that in Hebrews:

> *We have a great deal to say about this, and it's difficult to explain, since you have become slow to understand. For though by this time you ought to be teachers, you need someone to teach you again the basic principles of God's revelation. You need milk, not solid food. Now everyone who lives on milk is inexperienced with the message about righteousness, because he is an infant. But solid food is for*

*the mature—for those whose senses have been trained to
distinguish between good and evil.*
—Hebrews 5:11–14

Like the character Peter Pan escaping to Never Land so
he wouldn't have to grow up, Hebrews declares that far too
many Christians have never grown
into full adult maturity in spiritual
things. Spiritual maturity is never
measured by time but by a desire
to grow and by the obedience they
demonstrate. I believe the Christians
the author confronts in Hebrews
were under the heavy pressure of
persecution. Many of them were
spiritually immature and some of
them no doubt felt they could escape
persecution by repudiating their
faith in Jesus. Conversely, when the
time of persecution was over, they could become Christians
again and enjoy God's blessing once more.

> Spiritual maturity is measured by a desire to grow and by obedience.

One of the tactics the author of Hebrews uses is to remind
all these believers just what has happened to them. He speaks of
five occurrences that happened to those who became Christians
and who were then considering turning their backs on Jesus.
First, they have been enlightened. There is an ancient saying
that "when Jesus comes, the shadows depart." The darkness
experienced by the Jewish Christians had been shattered, and
the everlasting light had shone for them. Second, they tasted
the heavenly gift. God gave Himself to them in His Son. Third,
they became aware of the Holy Spirit, without whom no one
can be born from above. Fourth, they experienced the goodness
of God and discovered the truth in the Word of God. Fifth,

they experienced a foretaste of what it was to live in eternity as they tasted the powers of the age to come.

Inheritance and Development

What a glorious inheritance we have received as His children! Has this been your story? Are you anxious to grow? We have been granted a foundation that has made us so wealthy in so many ways. And yet, we see the reality of arrested spiritual development all over the church. Some people blame their work schedule, or their burdensome home life, or a thousand other things. For whatever reason, the truth is that many of us have just stopped growing in the Lord.

We see at least two indications of an arrested development in the lives of the Jewish Christians. First, *"For though by this time you ought to be teachers, you need someone to teach you again the basic principles of God's revelation. You need milk, not solid food"* (Hebrews 5:12). One indication of growth in spiritual things is the ability to help others understand the things of God. This includes the ability to advance in the Word, to share the gospel, to pray, and to witness. It also includes the ability to teach others the basics of Christian life and doctrine. But the sad truth is that most believers need someone to teach them the elementary truths of God's Word all over again.

The next indication of arrested development is the inability to tell good from evil. *"But solid food is for the mature—for those whose senses have been trained to distinguish between good and evil"* (Hebrews 5:14). The writer of Hebrews speaks of the message about righteousness. But the topic is not simply one of knowing what sin is and how to avoid it. It includes Christian behavior of every describable category.

Some Christians who lack growth in spiritual things are easily influenced by emotional appeal. In the area of mission support, they are swayed by tales of starving babies, disfigured lepers, and homeless mothers. Their missions dollar goes to those agencies that concentrate their advertisements along those lines. Some are fascinated by and easily caught up in theological fads that come and go on a cyclical basis, especially on the themes of eschatology, demonology, and angelology. Yet they have no real theological foundation or understanding of righteousness. The solid food of good, evil, and righteousness demand a discerning heart and experience with the message of righteousness, which those having arrested spiritual development do not possess.

> The solid food of good, evil, and righteousness demand a discerning heart and experience with the message of righteousness.

Meat or milk? The spiritually underdeveloped always thirst after milk, the baby food. They insist on spoon-fed, simple sermons that repeat the ideas they have grown accustomed to and to which they can automatically cry "amen" when they hear the familiar phrases of their favorite preacher. Certainly, easy-to-understand sermons are needed and the preaching of the gospel story will never go out of style, but we need to examine ourselves in light of what James says about only listening to the Word: *"Be doers of the word and not hearers only, deceiving yourselves"* (James 1:22). Far too many simply sit, soak, and sour, and become stunted spiritually.

The remedy is feeding on solid food, meat. *"Solid food is for the mature—for those whose senses have been trained to distinguish between good and evil"* (Hebrews 5:14). The mature are those who, by constant use or by a never-ending process, seek to understand and to do the will of God. These find real satisfaction and security in Christ. The missional leader must be a person of comprehension and learning, a person who has matured and yet is constantly seeking growth.

Reflections

1. How did Queen Esther show a discerning and comprehending spirit?

2. What were the indications of arrested development of the early Jewish Christians?

3. Solid food is for the mature. Who are the mature?

CHAPTER 10

A Missional Leader
Is an Excellent Conflict Manager

Many spiritual skills already outlined are imperative for the missional leader. Spiritual fruit must be present in the life of the missional leader, and this may well set him or her apart from the corporate or business leaders so often described in today's leadership books. It is a necessity for missional leaders to be persons of calling, vision, spiritual fruitfulness, prayer, and integrity. But the missional leader also must be a person of serious competency. Where does one receive the skills needed to be a true leader? For years, colleges and seminaries have struggled with how to teach leadership skills to students. Some believe leadership is an innate quality, part of a person's DNA, for one to truly be a leader. Most leaders recognize, however, that many of their skills and talents were learned, grown, and fashioned through an intentional process. As I have previously said, some personality types allow leadership to be developed faster in some persons than others. But calling, vision, and prayer can make a missional leader out of any personality type.

How Nehemiah Handled Conflict

What skills must be present for someone to be an effective missional leader? One of the first things to mention is an aptitude for conflict management. The Book of Nehemiah offers many examples on dealing with conflict. When Nehemiah began the journey to scout out the condition of Jerusalem, one of the important things he did in conflict management was to be quiet and hold his tongue: *"I got up at night and took a few men with me. I didn't tell anyone what my God had laid on my heart to do for Jerusalem. The only animal I took was the one I was riding"* (2:12). In this example, Nehemiah quietly spirited a few men away and did not let anyone know what was happening at that point in time. A missional leader knows when to confront and when to be quiet.

Nehemiah also chose the time for confrontation. *"I gave them this reply, 'The God of heaven is the One who will grant us success. We, His servants, will start building, but you have no share, right, or historic claim in Jerusalem'"* (2:20). The missional leader knows that confrontation sometimes is necessary, and very often a leader must be ready to confront, as distasteful and difficult as it may be. No one likes conflict, but we must never run from it either. To run from necessary discord is to delay the conflict and often exacerbate its inevitable result.

Nehemiah writes, *"They all plotted together to come and fight.... So we prayed to our God and stationed a guard because of them day and night"* (4:8–9). His reaction to intense opposition? Prayer. As established earlier, the missional leader is a person of serious prayer, and prayer must be seen as part of the skill of conflict management. We should never knowingly go into a confrontational situation without prayer!

Another instance of conflict and confrontation in Nehemiah regards people who were a part of the family of faith.

> "I became extremely angry when I heard their outcry and these complaints. . . .
>
> Then I said, 'What you are doing isn't right. Shouldn't you walk in the fear of our God?'" (5:6,9).
>
> "Then I replied to him, 'There is nothing to these rumors you are spreading; you are inventing them in your own mind'" (6:8).
>
> "I rebuked the nobles of Judah and said to them: 'What is this evil you are doing—profaning the Sabbath day?'" (13:17).

A missional leader must understand that conflict management must deal with the issue at hand. A large number of problems that churches, organizations, and families often deal with are smoke-screen issues. In other words, the true issue is often something much deeper or much more hidden. To correctly deal with conflict, one must handle the basic issue or question and avoid dealing with secondary or tertiary matters.

The Bible is a book about relationships, both divine and human. It includes glorious stories of joyous relationships, and it includes stories of devastating sadness in relationships gone wrong. Many accounts in Scripture reveal the reality of the snowball effect of sin in relationships, where innocent bystanders get caught up in a conflict not of their own choosing. Biblical examples of the snowball effect of sin and conflict date all the way back to Cain and Abel. They move up the history line to Jesus and His

A missional leader must understand that conflict management must deal with the issue at hand.

disciples, and Paul and Barnabas. Conflict is a reality in our human existence.

Dealing with Difficult People

Missional leaders often have to deal with difficult people. Marshall Shelly's book *Well-Intentioned Dragons* gives categories of difficult persons. For example, there is the Super Spiritual Bird Dog, a person always pointing out what the leader has not done. This is done in such a way as to make the leader feel not quite spiritual. There is the Wet Blanket, a person whose negative disposition is contagious. The Exploder, or the Sherman Tank, is a person who's lacking in diplomacy and always speaks with an explanation point rather than a period. This kind of person is always right, never wrong, but feels good after stating his or her opinions and releasing his or her emotions. The damage might be widespread among others, but the Exploder feels fine! Other categories include the Busybody, the Sniper (this is a person who avoids face-to-face contact but picks off leaders with pot shots in private conversations), the Bookkeeper, the Legalist, and the Termite (a person who works secretly).

> Pray diligently for God to reveal what is actually happening.

What are some things we can do to develop better conflict management skills with difficult people? First, consider the direct source involved in every confrontation. In my ministry I have found there is much to be learned from every situation. There are times I have been accused of things, or perhaps criticized for one thing or another, where the accuser spoke the truth. In fact, that is often the case. I try learning what I can from these brothers and sisters. If the criticism is well intentioned and has serious merit, the missional leader needs to pay careful attention to what they are saying.

Consider also the fact that smoke screens are often used to evade discussing the truth. This sort of thing happens a great deal in conflict situations. It is best to try clarifying the real issue. Pray diligently for God to reveal what is actually happening. If the confrontation is extremely emotional, remember that a kind, calm word will often diffuse the situation and allow the true issue to be discovered and discussed.

Some years ago, I pastored in another city where the church was across the street from one of our denominational seminaries. We were having a revival meeting, and I teasingly said the preacher was coming to "spit, slobber, and holler." He was very effusive and emotional. During the course of the sermon, the preacher made a rather strong statement about personal evangelism. He said if a Christian was not verbally sharing their faith, then they were backslidden.

The next day, a young woman who was enrolled in the seminary across the street came to visit me. She was visibly upset. In fact, she was more than upset, she was irate! Calmly, I tried to deal with her. She was very angry over the visiting preacher's statement of the prior evening. After I allowed her to vent for a time, she looked at me and said, "You're not taking up for me in my stance." Then she asked if I agreed with the pastor. I replied, "Yes, I do." At that very moment I felt the Holy Spirit revealing to me what the true issue was.

I asked her, "Is there someone God has been asking you to witness to, but you have refused?" Her emotions of anger and frustration turned to deep sadness. She began to weep. Finally, after having regained some composure, she confessed that God had led her to witness to a co-worker, but that she had failed in her duty to do so. She went on to confess that here she was angry at her pastor, and certainly angry at a visiting minister, when the true issue was that she had been disobedient.

Smoke screens are often the surface point of confrontation when there is a much deeper issue going on underneath. Missional leaders must pray for the discernment only God can give and the wisdom only God can grant so they will know what the crux of the matter really is. They must look for the underlying conflict that is much deeper than the smoke screen.

Remember, failure is not fatal. In a confrontational situation, there are times when we lose the argument. And there are times the consequences of our actions must be dealt with, and sometimes this makes us feel like failures. We have to see beyond the horizon of trouble and recognize God has not left us, even when we have failed or lost in a conflict situation, or when we feel friendless. Remember David, who was driven into hiding, Joseph and Paul, who were both imprisoned, and Jesus Christ, who was crucified for our guilt. Even in defeat, God's servants were not destroyed and neither are we. Part of the miracle of grace is that God uses broken vessels for His glory.

> **Failure is not fatal.**

Missional leaders who personify a nondefensive spirit of joy, grace, and generosity tend not to attract as many conflicts, or "dragons," as others. When the fruit of the Spirit is evident in the life of the missional leader, it becomes very clear whenever others violate that spirit. Even if they do, do not run from conflict. Face the situation with grace, yet with firmness. Ephesians 4:15 is an extremely important passage at this point. *"But speaking the truth in love, let us grow in every way into Him who is the head—Christ."* Speak the truth, but make sure it is stated in love. Speaking the truth without love leads to a coldhearted legalism. Speaking love without the truth leaves people with a coldhearted liberalism, bereft of direction and truth.

Prevent small conflicts from flaring up into holy wars. In the religious realm, absolutely nothing is bloodier than a religious war. Issues aren't just human squabbles anymore because everything is elevated to eternal and divine importance.

Mind-set, Motives, and Methods

Multiple skills are required for missional leaders because, if the leader is anything, he is a multitasker. Missional leaders must have serious skills to work with people and excel in conflict management. The missional leader constantly needs to review his or her mind-set, motive, and methodology.

During the Christmas season, an elderly woman decided it had become too difficult for her to get out and buy gifts for all her children and grandchildren. Wanting to continue to be a financial blessing to them, she decided to send money instead of buying gifts. She purchased Christmas cards for all the children and grandchildren and wrote a Merry Christmas greeting as well as a phrase she included, instructing them to "buy your own present this year."

She mailed the cards hoping this would be an acceptable alternative. But in January as she was cleaning up her desk, she was horrified to find the checks she had written to her children and grandchildren. She realized she sent out Christmas cards with the instructions for her family to buy their own gifts, without including the money for them to buy the gifts! The "buy your own present this year" certainly took on a different meaning.

I think we have done this very thing to our world. We tell them they need to change, yet we withhold a model of a New Testament believer who is able to alter his or her own life, perspective, behavior, and attitude. I also believe that we have withheld from our church world what missional leaders should

> We need to begin showing them through our changed lives how Christ can make a difference.

know about and exhibit in conflict management and everything else.

Paul was an apostle who portrayed a qualitative change in his behavior and worldview. Though he was far from perfect, he was able to present a message full of hope and substance. We need to stop telling our world to buy their own gift! We need to begin showing them through our changed lives how Christ can make a difference. There are many truths needed for the missional leader's life. While these principles will not make us perfect, they can and will dramatically alter our lives for spiritual victory, so we can say with Paul that what has happened to us has advanced the gospel.

> *Now I want you to know, brothers, that what has happened to me has actually resulted in the advancement of the gospel, so that it has become known throughout the whole imperial guard, and to everyone else, that my imprisonment is for Christ. Most of the brothers in the Lord have gained confidence from my imprisonment and dare even more to speak the message fearlessly. Some, to be sure, preach Christ out of envy and strife, but others out of good will. These do so out of love, knowing that I am appointed for the defense of the gospel; the others proclaim Christ out of rivalry, not sincerely, seeking to cause [me] trouble in my imprisonment. What does it matter? Just that in every way, whether out of false motives or true, Christ is proclaimed. And in this I rejoice. Yes, and I will rejoice because I know this will lead to my deliverance*

through your prayers and help from the Spirit of Jesus Christ. My eager expectation and hope is that I will not be ashamed about anything, but that now as always, with all boldness, Christ will be highly honored in my body, whether by life or by death.
—Philippians 1:12–20

At this point, even though Paul was waiting to be tried by Nero, he gave no indication of defeat. His body was bound, but his spirit was free. This powerful preacher of the gospel found himself in dire circumstances. His life moved from one of power and prominence in the Jewish hierarchy, hunting down newborn believers in Christ, to proclaiming Christ in prison. A dramatic conversion experience on the road to Damascus altered everything in the apostle's life. Instead of spending time with the intelligentsia, now he spent time with the rabble of the common mob. Instead of rubbing elbows with the rich and famous, now he spent time with the common people of the day.

Paul's circumstances had changed while writing the epistle to the Philippians. Now he finds himself imprisoned. The prisons of first-century Palestine were very different from the prisons of today, in that conditions then were extremely primitive and sparse. Despite the fact that circumstances had changed so dramatically for Paul, there were at least three areas over which he chose to remain in control. These areas are important to missional leaders, especially when conflict is experienced. What can be controlled?

Mind-set. More than anything else, Paul's desire as a missionary was to preach the gospel in Rome. If he could reach that city for Christ, it would mean reaching millions with the Christian message. Paul wanted to go to Rome as a preacher, but instead he went as a prisoner. To many, this would have looked like failure. But not to this apostle. Paul found joy, but certainly not in ideal physical circumstances. He found his joy in winning others to Christ.

> *Now I want you to know, brothers, that what has happened to me has actually resulted in the advancement of the gospel, so that it has become known throughout the whole imperial guard, and to everyone else, that my imprisonment is for Christ. Most of the brothers in the Lord have gained confidence from my imprisonment and dare even more to speak the message fearlessly.*
> —Philippians 1:12–14

The Philippian Christians were not to think that Paul's arrest and imprisonment stopped the gospel's progress. Quite the contrary. It's all a matter of mind-set. Instead of his chains hindering the gospel's progress, they had extended it. Little did the Romans realize the restraints affixed to his wrists would release Paul instead of bind him.

Imprisonment in chains gave Paul contact with the lost. He was shackled to a Roman soldier 24 hours a day, with the shift changing every 6 hours. This meant Paul could witness to at least four men each day. In other words, they didn't stand a chance of escaping listening to the good news of the gospel. Imagine yourselves as one of those soldiers chained to a man who prayed "without ceasing," who was constantly interviewing people about their spiritual condition, and who was repeatedly writing letters to Christians and churches throughout the empire.

Could it be that the situation we are in could be used for the glory of God?

The chains also gave Paul contact with the officials at Caesar's household. He was in Rome as an official prisoner, and his case was an important one. The Roman government was going to determine the official status of this new Christian sect. For Paul, this also was good, because it forced officials to study the doctrines of the Christian faith. Sometimes we all feel we're in chains. Could it be that the situation we are in could be used for the glory of God? Is it possible God has us in fetters for a reason? Could it be that what has happened has really served to advance the gospel, as in Paul's case? It all comes down to mind-set.

The secret is this. When one has the right kind of perspective, even negative circumstances can be seen as opportunities for the furtherance of the kingdom of God. One rejoices at what God is going to do instead of complaining about what God did not do.

Paul's chains not only gave him contact with the lost, they also gave courage to the Christians in Rome. Many of the believers in Rome took fresh courage when they saw Paul's faith and determination. They were far more bold to speak the Word. As Paul says, *"Most of the brothers in the Lord have gained confidence from my imprisonment and dare even more to speak the message fearlessly." Speak* in this context does not mean "preach." It refers to everyday conversation. Discouragement has a way of spreading, but so does encouragement. Because of Paul's joyful attitude, the believers in Rome took fresh courage and witnessed boldly for Christ.

We desperately need God's missional leaders to encourage our churches through fearless witnessing. As president of the Southern Baptist Convention, I lamented several times that Southern Baptists are best known not for what we stand for, but for what we are against. There are times we must stand against certain things, and we will continue to do so. But I have tried to reorient our public persona to show what we are *for*. I have tried to say we are for the life-changing, family-strengthening message of a personal relationship with Jesus Christ. Let us look at our roles as opportunities to give courage and encouragement to our fellow believers.

There are people around us who truly are believers, but they are in the doldrums and are in need of encouragement. They need to see how we handle the circumstances of our daily lives. They need to know that as missional leaders, we are not simply whining and complaining constantly about where we are, but rather we are seeking opportunities to bring glory to God through where we are.

Motives. There is the need to control our motives.

> *Some, to be sure, preach Christ out of envy and strife, but others out of good will. These do so out of love, knowing that I am appointed for the defense of the gospel; the others proclaim Christ out of rivalry, not sincerely, seeking to cause [me] trouble in my imprisonment. What does it matter? Just that in every way, whether out of false motives or true, Christ is proclaimed. And in this I rejoice.*

It is hard to believe anyone would oppose Paul, but there were believers in Rome doing just that. The churches there were divided, much like churches today. Some preached Christ sincerely, wanting to see people turn to the Lord. Some preached Christ insincerely, wanting to make the situation more difficult for Paul. The latter group was using the gospel to further their own selfish purposes. Perhaps they belonged to some legalistic wing of the church resisting Paul's ministry to the Gentiles and his emphasis on the grace of God as opposed to the obedience to Jewish law. Just as love and unity go together, envy and strife seem to go together.

Paul's aim was to glorify Christ and to bring people into Christ's kingdom. The purpose of His critics, however, was to promote themselves and to win a following of their own. Their motive was perverse. Instead of asking, "Have you trusted Christ?" they asked, "Whose side are you on, ours or Paul's?" Unfortunately, this kind of religious activity can be seen very clearly even today. The people who practice it should realize they are only hurting themselves.

We all need constantly to check our motives. Why do we do what we do? When we have the correct motive, we look on our critics as another opportunity for the furtherance of the gospel. Like a faithful soldier, Paul was appointed for the preaching of the gospel. He was able to rejoice, not in the selfishness of his critics, but in the fact that Christ was still being preached. There was no envy in Paul's heart, and it mattered not that some were for him and some against him. All that mattered was the preaching of the gospel of Jesus Christ.

As a missional and denominational leader, I can say that many people in our denomination think it belongs to them. Before your mind goes to any one group, I assure you there are multiple groups feeling they own this Convention. It belongs to them. This belief leads to a mistaken notion that because they own it, they can

Who owns the church?

control it. Control leads to a lack of perspective. I assure you, there have been times I felt the Convention belonged to me. It does not! We should all seek to influence our movement in a positive way when we can, but we are fools to think we own and therefore control any part of the denomination.

The same thing happens in churches. Who owns the church? How many churchgoers by their actions show they think the church belongs to them? It is time to check motives! It is extremely important our motives be pure and right. Obviously, where there is disunity in the body of Christ, it breaks the heart of God. Are we here to serve the Lord and promote His agenda, or to promote ourselves and our own ideological beliefs?

There is an often-told story about John Wesley and George Whitefield. It is a matter of historical record that they disagreed on many doctrinal matters. Both of them were very successful, preaching to thousands of people and seeing multitudes come to Christ. It is reported that someone asked Wesley if he expected to see Whitefield in heaven, and the evangelist responded, "No, I do not." "Then you do not think Whitefield is a converted man?" "Of course he is a converted man!" Wesley said, "I do not expect to see him in heaven because he will be so close to the throne of God, and I will be so far away, that I will not be able to see him!" Though he differed with his brother in some matters, Wesley did not have any envy in his heart, nor did he seek to oppose Whitefield's ministry.

Criticism is hard to take, particularly when we are in difficult circumstances, as Paul was. How was the apostle able to rejoice and have correct motives even in the face of such diverse criticism? He possessed the mind of Christ.

Methods. Paul's confidence is expressed beautifully when he says,

> *Yes, and I will rejoice because I know this will lead to my deliverance through your prayers and help from the Spirit of Jesus Christ. My eager expectation and hope is that I will not be ashamed about anything, but that now as*

always, with all boldness, Christ will be highly honored
in my body, whether by life or by death.
—Philippians 1:18–20

His expectation is that everything that happens will, in some way, turn out to bring glory to the Lord. Is this our expectation, even in conflict?

Interestingly, Paul's hope was that everything happening through his experience would be done in such a way that he would not be ashamed. I believe the apostle is speaking here not only of mind-set and motive, but also of methodology. Most commentators believe this statement to be a broad one referring to Paul's appearance before the authorities for the final disposition of his case. It should be our earnest prayer that nothing we do, say, or think brings reproach upon the cause of Christ. Those of us who seek to be missional leaders should hope for this beyond anything else.

> It should be our earnest prayer that nothing we do, say, or think brings reproach to the cause of Christ.

We must seek daily God's Holy Spirit's guidance so in no way will we be ashamed or bring shame to Him. I believe this means we need to check our methodology. Some say, "I don't care what your method is, just as long as your message is right and as long as the end result is right." This is wrong. I believe that some methods are unworthy of the gospel. They are cheap and sleazy, whereas the gospel is a costly message requiring the death of God's only Son. We must constantly evaluate what we are doing in the Lord's name and how we are doing it. Our methodology has to be pleasing to God. A question we should all ask in whatever we do is, "Does it bring shame upon Christ in any form or fashion?"

Circumstances can change, and they can find us in very difficult situations. There is nothing wrong with trying to get out of a bad situation. It is incumbent upon every believer and leader, however, to look for ways to bring glory to the Lord, even in the midst of difficult and sometimes even terrible settings. Is our motive one of pure devotion to Christ? Are we doing what we do for His glory or for our own credit? Do we hide envy in our hearts? I believe it is time to check our mind-sets, motives, and methodologies.

When missional leaders exhibit competency in conflict management skills, the result is things happening for the kingdom of God. Not only do good things happen, but the Enemy realizes it is God who empowers the church to do the work. Isn't it time for our world—and the gods of this world—to be intimidated by the church and lose their confidence when they see the great things God wants to do actually happen? Wouldn't my reader agree it is time for a revival to occur among God's people so the world recognizes the good things happening could only be explained because of the hand of God? I hope you agree.

Reflections

1. What skills should a missional leader have in order to be effective?

2. How did Nehemiah handle conflict and confrontation?

3. What steps can we take to develop better conflict skills with difficult people?

4. Who owns the church? Explain.

CHAPTER 11

A Missional Leader
Is a Person of Courage

The missional leader recognizes that fine line between courage and stupidity and is careful to stay on the "courage" side of that line. Courage is one of the greatest characteristics of true leaders and is vital. A sign of courage in leaders is that they do not leave when opposition arises. Nehemiah shows us the courage missional leaders desperately need:

> *When Sanballat the Horonite, Tobiah the Ammonite official, and Geshem the Arab heard [about this], they mocked and despised us, and said, "What is this you're doing? Are you rebelling against the king?" I gave them this reply, "The God of heaven is the One who will grant us success. We, His servants, will start building, but you have no share, right, or historic claim in Jerusalem."*
> —Nehemiah 2:19–20

> *I went to the house of Shemaiah son of Delaiah, son of Mehetabel, who was restricted [to his house]. He said: Let us meet at the house of God inside the temple. Let us shut*

the temple doors because they are coming to kill you. They
are coming to kill you tonight!

But I said, "Should a man like me run away? How
can I enter the temple and live? I will not go." I realized
that God had not sent him, because of the prophecy he
spoke against me. Tobiah and Sanballat had hired him.
He was hired, so that I would be intimidated, do as he
suggested, sin, and get a bad reputation, in order that they
could discredit me.
—Nehemiah 6:10–13

Nehemiah would not be intimidated, and he refused to run in
the face of threatening opposition. His courage was not found
in some false sense of bravado, but rather in a deep and abiding
conviction that *"the God of heaven . . . will grant us success."*

Missional leaders need that kind of confidence and
courage. Today, many live in the spirit of fear and defeat that
has destroyed the lives and the effectiveness of too many leaders.
Yes, we live in the midst of spiritual warfare. The Evil One will
do everything he can to discourage, to bring a spirit of fear, and
to defeat the work of the Lord. Missional leaders depending on
the power of the Lord can be people
of courage. Remember the words
of David who stood before Goliath
and said, *"I come against you in the*
name of the LORD of Hosts, the God of
Israel's armies" (1 Samuel 17:45). He
believed in the power of the name of
the Lord.

> The call of the Lord transcends our own weaknesses, abilities, and possibilities.

The missional leader has the
power and purpose of God within.
Every person, regardless of innate
leadership skills, has the privilege of

knowing the call of the Lord transcends our own weaknesses, abilities, and possibilities. In other words, the missional leader has the greatest of all advantages, because he or she knows they do not have to make up or manipulate some kind of inner feeling for success.

People who might consider themselves missional leaders too often become caught up in conflict and difficulty and begin to despair. They cannot see beyond the horizon of trouble. When difficulty came to Nehemiah, he saw beyond the difficulty to the task God set before him. Our Lord Jesus had this tremendous capacity to look beyond the horizon of trouble.

> *"Simon, Simon, look out! Satan has asked to sift you like wheat. But I have prayed for you that your faith may not fail. And you, when you have turned back, strengthen your brothers."*
>
> *"Lord," he told Him, "I'm ready to go with You both to prison and to death!"*
>
> *"I tell you, Peter," He said, "the rooster will not crow today until you deny three times that you know Me!"*
> —Luke 22:31–34

Knowing the power of God and seeing Him work through one's own life gives one the courage to move forward, even during difficult times. This is truly the difference between good leaders and great leaders.

Our rich heritage encourages us

Examples of courage in Scripture are rich and plentiful. This courage was exhibited by Joseph as he refused moral compromise with Potiphar's wife (Genesis 39:9). Moses portrayed this courage when he confronted the people about the golden calf and smashed the tablets at the base of the mountain (Exodus 32:19). Caleb displayed it when risking his life by giving the minority report recommending taking possession of Canaan (Numbers 13:30). Even Balaam showed courage when refusing to speak against Israel to Balak (Numbers 24:10). Joshua often revealed courage in his leadership of Israel as they conquered the Promised Land (Joshua 11:6). Deborah, the judge, exhibited great courage by taking the role of leadership not customarily given to women (Judges 4:4–5). Daniel and his friends Hananiah, Mishael, and Azariah (the Hebrew names for Shadrach, Meshach, and Abednego) all displayed tremendous courage by standing faithful to the Lord during the reign of Nebuchadnezzar. Hosea portrayed courage as he obeyed the Lord in His unusual command to marry the adulteress (Hosea 3:1). Both Mary and Joseph were great examples of courage as they followed the will of the Lord (Matthew 1). John the Baptist was certainly courageous when he confronted Herod and his immorality in Matthew 14:4.

> Even in the worst of times, the missional leader is to be a person of courage.

Is courage not what transformed 12 ordinary men, followers of Christ for three years, to become world changers? Is this not the factor that gave Stephen, the young deacon, the courage to stand strong for his belief? Even when being stoned to death, Stephen displayed courage and the spirit of Christ when he asked the Lord not to charge the betrayers and murderers with sin as they killed him (Acts 7:51–60). And of course there is the Apostle Paul. He wasn't afraid to stand up to the municipal authorities, the Jewish antagonists, or anyone else who might want to curtail his ministry. Why all these examples of courage? Because even in the worst of times the missional leader is to be a person of courage.

October 13, 2006, began as a somewhat normal day in my life. My wife and I had spent the night in Charlotte, having traveled from a preaching engagement the previous evening. She was going to drive back to Greenville, our home, and I was going to fly out of the Charlotte airport to a speaking engagement in Indiana. That morning, as we were preparing to leave, I received a phone call from a dear friend, a physician in our church, who had been reviewing some tests performed on my daughter, Melissa. Time seemed to stand still. My friend told me Melissa had Hodgkin's lymphoma. He said the tests were not totally conclusive, but based on his years of experience, he knew that was what it was. My daughter was experiencing no pain or difficulty, but she had had some swollen lymph nodes in her shoulder. Regardless of medical etiquette, my friend wanted me to be the one to tell my daughter the news.

This phone call began a six-month journey of treatments to rid my daughter's body of this cancer. The fact that this illness befell my daughter four months after I was elected president of the Southern Baptist Convention was for me a clear realization that the Evil One wished to distract and to destroy joy in my family's life. Cancer is not a rare disease. Multiple thousands experience this in their own lives and in the lives of family members. I imagine many reading this book have had to deal with this dreaded reality in their lives. My family is certainly not immune from difficulty, and I am well aware the Evil One wishes to use anything and everything to keep believers from experiencing the power and passion of Christ.

I've often said that it's a father's responsibility to protect his daughters. I am the father of three precious daughters and am passionately committed to caring for them and protecting them. But this was something I could not protect my daughter from. I could make sure she had the best care and the greatest support that a family, friends, and a church could provide. Today, Melissa is cancer free, living a wonderful life, and has experienced great growth spiritually due to what happened in her life. We can truly say that Romans 8:28 is still applicable: *"We know that all things work together for the good of those who love God: those who are called according to His purpose."*

We tried to face our trial with courage. The missional leader is a person of courage who lets nothing dissuade her from what God has called her to do. Winston Churchill had that same kind of spirit. As a young man, he attended Harrow Preparatory School. When he was prime minister, Churchill was invited to return to Harrow to speak to the student body. Attempting to prepare the students for the prime minister's visit, the headmaster told them to listen carefully because Churchill was one of England's most eloquent orators. When the morning came for Churchill to speak, he acknowledged the introduction given him by the headmaster. Looking sternly at the young student body, he scowled: "Young gentlemen, never give up! Never give up! Never give up! Never! Never! Never! Never! Never!" And then he sat down. It was a speech the students would never forget.

The issue of courage can never be underestimated. It shows an inner strength—an intestinal fortitude that gives a leader the ability to make the hard choices, the hard call, and to live with the consequences of one's decisions. The missional leader can depend on the call and direction of God and therefore is not simply making decisions out of a personal agenda. This kind of spiritually based courage yields great results, as Scripture all over affirms. We have a great need for missional leaders possessed of a profound spiritual courage.

However obscure, one of the greatest passages in the New Testament showing the end result of one's strong convictions is found in the nineteenth chapter of the Book of Acts.

> *Then some of the itinerant Jewish exorcists attempted to pronounce the name of the Lord Jesus over those who had evil spirits, saying, "I command you by the Jesus whom Paul preaches!" Seven sons of Sceva, a Jewish chief priest, were doing this. The evil spirit answered them, "Jesus I know, and Paul I recognize—but who are you?" Then the man who had the evil spirit leaped on them, overpowered them all, and prevailed against them, so that they ran out of that house naked and wounded.*
> —Acts 19:13–16

In this passage, we see seven Jews, all sons of chief priest Sceva, trying to cast out demons. They are confronted with a very poignant question from the demons themselves: *"Who are you?"* The demons knew Jesus and had heard about Paul, but they did not know these itinerant exorcists. It is obvious from the context of the passage that the only way demonic forces would know the names of individual believers is due to a legacy of commitment of those believers to Christ. The demons did not know these others who were attempting to cast them out. Leonard Ravenhill once asked the question, "Is your name known in hell?" We should all ask this question of ourselves, because if we truly believe what we say we believe, there will be a strength of conviction that is known both in heaven and in hell.

When we are truly on the Lord's side, then even the demons of hell know our name. Is your name known in hell?

Do the angels of darkness tremble because of your reputation as a winner of souls and a prayer warrior in the kingdom? Do they tremble because of your tireless efforts in encouraging and discipling other believers? I want to be a missional leader of courage and of whom the Lord is proud. I want my name to be known both in heaven and hell.

Reflections

1. How did Nehemiah model the characteristic of courage?

2. Sometimes missional leaders cannot see beyond the horizon of trouble. How does one move forward even during difficult times?

3. Is your name known in both heaven and hell?

CHAPTER 12

A Missional Leader
Is a Person of Commitment

What is normal? What is abnormal? There is an old adage that says, "All the world is strange, except you and me, and sometimes I'm not so sure about you." It doesn't hurt to take a hard look at ourselves from time to time. During a visit to the mental asylum, a visitor asked the director what the criterion was that defined whether or not a patient should be institutionalized. "Well," said the director, "we fill up a bathtub, and then we offer a teaspoon, a teacup and a bucket to the patient and ask him or her to empty the bathtub." "Oh, I understand," said the visitor. "A normal person would use the bucket because it's bigger than the spoon or the teacup." "No." said the director. "A normal person would pull the plug. Do you want a bed near the window?"

It is extremely important the missional leader understand what a normal commitment is. We have previously discussed the issue of charisma, that ability to commit to a cause or task that is even greater than ourselves. We have talked about vision, and we have talked about courage. In thinking about commitment, how committed should a person be to any given task? As I said before, there is a fine line between courage and stupidity. There is also a fine line between commitment and fanaticism. Someone described a fanatic as "someone who is more committed than me." If that is true, we need far more fanatics in our churches and Christian organizations. The missional leader must be a person of authentic commitment.

Nehemiah was a committed man, even in the face of opposition from those who did not want him to rebuild the walls of Jerusalem.

> *When Sanballat the Horonite, Tobiah the Ammonite official, and Geshem the Arab heard [about this], they mocked and despised us, and said, "What is this you're doing? Are you rebelling against the king?" I gave them this reply, "The God of heaven is the One who will grant us success. We, His servants, will start building, but you have no share, right, or historic claim in Jerusalem."*
> —Nehemiah 2:19–20

Nehemiah was willing to pay the price, whatever that was, to remain committed to his task. Commitment goes beyond courage. Courage is the ability to stand up to the enemy. But commitment is the willingness to pay the daily price of sacrifice. Commitment is proving courage by working diligently to do the task. Nehemiah and the people of God were all committed to the effort to rebuild the walls. *"So we rebuilt the wall until the entire wall was joined together up to half its height, for the people had the will to keep working"* (Nehemiah 4:6). That is commitment! Like courage, commitment is not based on an innate sense of confidence in one's own strength. That, in fact, would be hubris, not commitment.

Changing Our Perspective

I believe we need a new perspective that gives us a confidence in the power of the Lord. This perspective will make missional leaders people of commitment. One of the great truths we all need to learn is that it is not the circumstances of life but rather our perspective on life that determines the outcome of our life. We spend great effort changing the circumstances of our daily existence, but rarely do we seek to change our perspective. There are some, I know, who go to great extremes trying to be positive in their outlook on life. I am always amused at those who choose to exhibit a positive attitude while ignoring reality.

> It is not the circumstances of life but rather our perspective on life that determines the outcome of our life.

Robert Schuller tells of the father who took his son duck hunting. The father had boasted to the son that he was the greatest hunter in the world. Finally, on a cold winter morning, they went duck hunting and sat for quite a while waiting to find some ducks. Finally, one lonely winged waterfowl wafted its way across the sky. The father stood to shoot and in so doing missed totally. Then the father looked at the son and said, "Son, you have just witnessed a miracle. There flies a dead duck."

We all know people who go to extremes concocting a new perspective on life, even while ignoring reality to do so. I do believe we can have a positive approach to life. But our proactive approach has to be one based on the truth of God's power to transform, and on our hope enabling us to serve a living Savior. When we view life in this manner, we become "possibility people." It is the state of mind being fully alive. Fully alive people find enjoyment in what others regard as drudgery or duty. They don't have to, they want to. They are aware of the thorns but concentrate on the roses. Each day seems to have a newness about it, and fully alive people eagerly await new insights. Our need for missional leaders who are fully alive and who are possibility people is desperate.

Let me now add to the story I was telling earlier about Caleb and his exploits in Canaan.

> *Joshua son of Nun and Caleb son of Jephunneh, who were among those who scouted out the land, tore their clothes and said to the entire Israelite community: "The land we passed through and explored is an extremely good land. If the LORD is pleased with us, He will bring us into this land, a land flowing with milk and honey, and give it to us. Only don't rebel against the LORD, and don't be afraid of the people of the land, for we will devour them. Their protection has been removed from them, and the LORD is with us. Don't be afraid of them!"*
> —Numbers 14:6–9

Caleb, of the tribe of Judah, was one of the 12 scouts sent to spy out the land of Canaan. They returned reporting a bountiful land, but a land that inhabited by a very powerful and warlike people. While most of the scouts said, "We can't do it," Joshua and Caleb said, *"We can certainly conquer!"* (13:30) Caleb typifies a possibility person with a *"different spirit"* (14:24), of one who followed God completely. Let us look deeper into the character of this man who had a unique perspective and vision in life.

A possibility person has a faith that trusts in God's power. Of course, his faith in what God can do is supplemented by a spiritual common sense and a godly learning. Caleb *"quieted the people"* (13:30) and told them of his surveillance of the land. He was not a person speaking out of ignorance. No, his surveillance of the land gave him a unique perspective.

Christians who have experienced God's touch know God's power and are not afraid to use it. Caleb said, *"If the LORD is pleased with us, He will bring us into this land, a land flowing with milk and honey, and give it to us"* (14:8). We need missional leaders like Caleb who have learned the Word of God, applied it, and allowed it to transform their lives. We need people who are not afraid to learn and grow. A possibility person has a faith that is knowledgeable and well-informed, and is someone who is fully alive and knows what God can do.

Caleb had an expectant faith. Speaking to the Israelites of the Promised Land, he affirmed, *"We can certainly conquer it!"* (13:30), and *"He will bring us into this land"* (14:8). In 14:24, God confirmed Caleb's desire and responded, *"I will bring him into the land where he has gone, and his descendants will inherit it"* (14:24). He knew God was able, and with that knowledge he stepped out in faith. Though the people rejected his advice at first, and even went so far as to attempt to stone him, he was courageous in his faith and allowed nothing to dissuade him.

The American church needs people with that kind of expectancy and resolve. It's like the story of the colonel in World War II who said to his troops, "The enemy is in front of us, in back of us, to the left and to the right. They can't get away from us this time." We need missional leaders with this level of expectant, committed faith. We need to step out in faith and let God do His work. We need a new perspective as churches, groups, families, and individuals.

Caleb was a man of great courage. He said, *"Don't be afraid of the people of the land, for we will devour them. Their protection has been removed from them, and the LORD is with us. Don't be afraid of them!"* (14:9). Caleb had a faith that was well-informed and trusting in God's power, and thus he knew what God could do. He was so excited in what God could do that he would have charged hell with a water pistol. A fully alive person is a person of this brand of courage.

Fully Alive to Possibility

A fully alive person is honored by the Lord for his faithfulness and consistency. God observed that Caleb had *"a different spirit and has followed Me completely"* (14:24). Literally, this means he had another spirit, a spirit of obedience. He was a possibility person, and God honors possibility persons. Because of Caleb's different spirit, God blessed him with the fulfillment of His promises. In the Book of Joshua, chapter fourteen, we read of the fulfillment of that covenant when Caleb was given the land promised to him (14:14). It is interesting to note that when he was over 80 years old, Caleb affirmed he was as strong as he was in his youth and still well able to fight for the Lord. Caleb was honored by God for his faithfulness and consistency.

> We need to be ready and willing for whatever God wants.

Will the Lord of Hosts honor us in such a way? Our Father wants us to be ready to serve Him, and to do so in faithfulness and consistency. Years ago, there was a young man who could barely read or write. He received a draft notice from the draft board. While he had difficulty with the form, he finally wrote a note at the bottom and sent it back and said, "Dear Uncle Sam, I don't understand all these here questions. Let me just say one thing, if you're ready, I'm ready." God wants His people to be like that too. Though we may not understand everything about what He will do with us, we need to be ready and willing for whatever God wants.

The missional leadership and commitment of Nehemiah produced tremendous results. The wall around Jerusalem was completed in 52 days (6:15). The tremendous task of rebuilding several miles of wall without modern-day equipment was a formidable one. But with the commitment Nehemiah and his followers exhibited, the wall was completed. The results? Not only were Jerusalem's walls of protection restored, but its effect on the enemies was very dramatic. *"When all our enemies heard this, all the surrounding nations were intimidated and lost their confidence, for they realized that this task had been accomplished by our God"* (6:16).

Nehemiah's commitment to the task led him to be quite creative. Nehemiah 4:17 shows how he led the people to be creative in doing their work. *"The laborers who carried the loads worked with one hand and held a weapon with the other."* In the same chapter, Nehemiah continued his creative leadership by putting in place a system for pulling the people together at a time of special need (19–23).

God affirmed Nehemiah's commitment, courage, and creativity. We have seen how God affirmed the leadership of Caleb and his courage and commitment. According to the parable of the talents, He wishes to do the same for all of us.

"For it is just like a man going on a journey. He called his own slaves and turned over his possessions to them. To one he gave five talents; to another, two; and to another, one—to each according to his own ability. Then he went on a journey. Immediately the man who had received five talents went, put them to work, and earned five more. In the same way the man with two earned two more. But the

man who had received one talent went off, dug a hole in the ground, and hid his master's money. After a long time the master of those slaves came and settled accounts with them. The man who had received five talents approached, presented five more talents, and said, 'Master, you gave me five talents. Look, I've earned five more talents.' His master said to him, 'Well done, good and faithful slave! You were faithful over a few things; I will put you in charge of many things. Share your master's joy!' Then the man with two talents also approached. He said, 'Master, you gave me two talents. Look, I've earned two more talents.' His master said to him, 'Well done, good and faithful slave! You were faithful over a few things; I will put you in charge of many things. Share your master's joy!' Then the man who had received one talent also approached and said, 'Master, I know you. You're a difficult man, reaping where you haven't sown and gathering where you haven't scattered seed. So I was afraid and went off and hid your talent in the ground. Look, you have what is yours.' But his master replied to him, 'You evil, lazy slave! If you knew that I reap where I haven't sown and gather where I haven't scattered, then you should have deposited my money with the bankers. And when I returned I would have received my money back with interest. So take the talent from him and give it to the one who has 10 talents. For to everyone who has, more will be given, and he will have more than enough. But from the one who does not have, even what he has will be taken away from him. And throw this good-for-nothing slave into the outer darkness. In that place there will be weeping and gnashing of teeth.'"

—Matthew 25:14–30

This parable teaches that we can waste our opportunity for God. We can waste our opportunity for ministering significantly to others, and when there is no commitment to the task, that is what happens. This parable also instructs us to have a great faith in the good character of our God. This story of the talents has three scenes: The distribution of the gifts, the use made of the gifts, and the day of reckoning.

On the distribution of the gifts, every servant received something. Every one has some talent. These "talents" were actually sums of money and, considering the times, the talents represented a large sum of money. Every Christian has been given something, and so it is with us. These talents represent the powers and means God has entrusted to His people for carrying on His kingdom work in the world today. They also include the gifts that the Apostle Paul enumerates as being distributed by the Holy Spirit (Romans 12; 1 Corinthians 12–14; and Ephesians 4). Perhaps it could be said these talents represent the variety of talents and gifts found in the body of Christ: the gospel itself, the truths Christ preached, the training received, the Holy Spirit energy that is available, the education we have, the skill that has been acquired, along with Christian experience, health, wealth, time, opportunities, and effectiveness in preaching and teaching. God has entrusted to us all the gifts and endowments of the Holy Spirit.

> God has entrusted to us all the gifts and endowments of the Holy Spirit.

But while every servant received some gift, all did not receive the same or equal gifts. Our gifts also vary. No two of us are alike. We are born with varying abilities and are born again with varying spiritual gifts. We are unequal also in the opportunities we have for developing our gifts. Some are raised in Christian homes. Some are of modest means while others seem to have unlimited means. Some are homeschooled and some are sent to the finest and most prestigious of schools.

These talents, whether few or many, came to the servants as a gift. Not one is deserving of honor above another. This to say that the greater-gifted servant is not to glory in the presence of the servant with fewer gifts. Nor is the lesser gifted to feel inferior. It is not the wealth of our endowment that entitles us to honor, but rather the use we make of the endowment. Therefore, as these individuals come from the presence of their master, each with his gift, one is as much entitled to honor as another.

Surrendering Our Talents

Regarding the use of these gifts, how do the slaves treat the talents their master put into their hands? In the parable, the man with two talents and the man with five talents both go to work eagerly and wholeheartedly. They make up their minds they are going to do their best to be worthy of their master's confidence. The third slave, however, was different. Probably the man of one talent did not leave his master thinking he would do nothing with the money. He was doubtless quite thrilled over the confidence placed in him; that is, until he compared his gifts with those of the others. It was then he lost his courage and went back home. He did not call in his friends to help him party and squander the talent. He just slipped out into the back yard and buried it.

Why did the third man do this? He said he was afraid, and it is easy to see what he feared. He was filled with dread he might not be able to show big returns with his one talent, as his more gifted counterparts had done. He was afraid to wound his own pride. If he could not be captain of the team, he would not play at all. If he could not be first violin, it was not worth joining the orchestra. If he could not be the largest contributor to his church, he would give nothing. If he could not sing as well or better than anybody in the choir, he would simply sit in silence. We rob and torture ourselves by fearing to wound our own pride!

The third man was also afraid of work. He was proud, and he was also lazy. How much of our failure in matters of spirituality can be accounted for by sheer laziness? There are many tasks that need accomplishing, and we know we can and ought to do them, but it is just too much trouble. Missional leaders do not want to become the twin brother or sister of the one-talent servant.

This man counted his single talent as being of no great importance. Evidently he assumed his one talent was not really needed. But every talent is needed in the divine economy. He failed to appreciate that every talent is precious in the eyes of God. A Christian businessman was traveling in Korea accompanied by a missionary. One day he saw a young man in a field by the side of the road pulling a rude plow, while an older man guided the handles. The businessman was amused and took a snapshot of the scene. The layman said to the missionary guide, "I suppose these people are very poor."

> Every talent is needed in the divine economy. Every talent is precious in the eyes of God.

"Yes," was the very quiet reply. "Those two men happen to be Christians. When their church was being built, they were eager to give something toward it but they had no money. So they decided to sell their one and only ox and gave the proceeds to the church. This spring they are pulling the plow themselves." The businessman was silent for a few moments and then he said, "That must have been a real sacrifice." The missionary's reply was that they did not call it a sacrifice. Instead, they were rather proud that they had the ox to give.

This third slave lacked gumption—the faith and courage to take a risk. He lacked commitment. He decided he'd be cautious and play it safe. He is like those who never "go for broke" in order that they might succeed in a business or professional venture. If we would do something significant, we must take the risk of failure and trust God to come through on His promises. We must expose ourselves to the peril of embarrassment and loss if we ever plan to do anything worthwhile. What if Abraham played it safe and refused to risk leaving his home and going to a far country for God? Moses wanted to play it safe and tried every excuse in the book to avoid responding to God's call. Finally he took the risk and became the great deliverer.

We can all be grateful that Jesus did not play it safe. If Paul and the other apostles had played it safe and had never taken the risk of failure, we probably would have never known about the gospel of Jesus Christ. Many people think their talent is so small it does not matter, and therefore they neglect responding to their opportunities. When we do this, we become a sibling of the one-talent man.

At the day of reckoning, there is only one test. The Master asks no questions as to our cleverness. He asks no questions as to the slaves' success. The one question He asks is this: "Have you been faithful?" The five-talent man had increased his store a hundred percent. The two-talent man had done the same. But these men were not commended for that reason—they were commended because they had been faithful. Whoever does his or her best is rated at the level of perfection. The Bible speaks of certain saints as perfect—Noah, for instance. But that does not mean Noah was faultless. It only means he was wholehearted, and that he did his best.

There is a twofold reward promised to those doing the best they can. The person who uses what he or she has will find his or her gifts increased, while those refusing to use them will find them decreasing little by little until they vanish. This is true in every department of life. We can double our capital (talents) by faithfulness and commitment. We can improve our own usefulness and fruitfulness. We can have twice as much if we are reliable and trustworthy in using what God has placed in our hands.

If using is *increasing*, it is equally sure that neglecting is *losing*. This is the law of life. If one wants to destroy all accumulated knowledge and learning, it is not necessary to burn up the libraries in the world. What is required, instead, is to leave them entirely alone. To destroy the sweetest marriage relationship, the husband and wife do not need to argue. What they need to do is neglect each other. If one wants to abandon a fine friendship, insult and threat is not needed. All that needs to be done is to neglect your friend.

If we are faithful, there is the additional reward of receiving our Lord's approval and praise. We receive the acceptance of God when we believe in and follow Jesus Christ as Savior and Lord. He receives us, forgives us of our sins, and accepts us into the body of Christ and the kingdom of God. We can have His approval and His praise if we are faithful in the use of the gifts He confers on us. We can enter into the joy of the Lord both in the here and in the hereafter. We can hear the Master say, "Well done." This parable of the talents teaches us the joy of doing good and being God's love to others. Ours can be the joy of seeing people come to know Jesus Christ as Savior. Ours can be the joy of becoming what God wants us to be.

Missional leaders are people of commitment who complete the task because it comes from God And so does the power.

Reflections

1. Nehemiah was a committed man even in the face of opposition. What kind of perspective will make missional leaders people of commitment?

2. What is a possibility person?

3. Explain how Caleb had an expectant faith. How can we have the same resolve?

4. What does this mean: "Using is increasing and neglecting is losing"?

CHAPTER 13

A Missional Leader
Is a Person of Communication

I do enjoy the sometimes scintillating repartee between men and women. Often the interchange deals with the issue of communication. For example, an actual newspaper ad was printed as follows: "For sale by owner: complete set of *Encyclopaedia Britannica*. 45 volumes. Excellent condition. $1,000 or best offer. No longer needed. Got married last month. Husband knows everything."

Despite attendant difficulties, the missional leader is committed to communication. The Old Testament Book of Nehemiah is the story of a missional leader communicating with the Lord, with those in authority over him, and with the people of God. Nehemiah knew how to connect with various constituencies. In John Kramp's book, *On Track Leadership*, he rightly says, "Visioning and personal planning create a picture of the destination and a general plan to get there. However, only communication moves that picture from the mind of the leader to the minds of those who board the passenger car through enlistment."

The ability to communicate clearly, succinctly, and powerfully is one of the greatest characteristics in missional leadership. There are thousands of leaders in our land who have tremendous ideas, yet many lack the communication skills necessary to transmit the information to those they seek to lead.

The story of Nehemiah's communication with the king and his fellow Israelites is found in the second chapter of Nehemiah.

> So I said to them, "You see the trouble we are in. Jerusalem lies in ruins and its gates have been burned down. Come, let's rebuild Jerusalem's wall, so that we will no longer be a disgrace." I told them how the gracious hand of my God had been on me, and what the king had said to me. They said, "Let's start rebuilding," and they were encouraged to [do] this good work.
> —Nehemiah 2:17–18

Nehemiah also communicated with his enemies.

> I gave them this reply, "The God of heaven is the One who will grant us success. We, His servants, will start building, but you have no share, right, or historic claim in Jerusalem."
> —Nehemiah 2:20

"Truthing" in Love

Sometimes Nehemiah's communication was positive, and sometimes it was confrontational. There are times when the missional leader has to do both. In fact, one of the great marks of the missional leader is, he or she knows how to have balance in this area. There should be times of positive encouragement as well as times of exhortation.

In my experience as a pastor, I have tried to learn this balance. There is a time to be serious and a time to be funny. There is a time to balance both work and play. The spiritual and the practical need to be balanced as well. Sometimes one needs to be with others and sometimes it is best to be alone. Communication involves the same kind of balance. There are times I felt the need to publicly thank my people in effusive ways.

Recently, for example, after I had witnessed scores of volunteers at work in one of our Single Mom's Oil Change Saturdays, I could not help but express my deep appreciation for their sacrifice in ministering to more than 100 single mothers and their families. Great ministry had been done, many souls were blessed, and relationships had been built. I wanted my people to know how deeply thankful I was for their efforts.

> **Praise should be done publicly, but criticism of individuals should be done privately.**

On the other hand, there have been times I felt the need to be very stern with my people. For example, when I have been seriously disappointed in our evangelistic outreach, I have felt the need and the calling from God to speak to our people quite strongly. Balance is the key! When people know you love them, they listen to exhortation, even criticism.

Sometimes the missional leader must communicate on a private level using the same kind of balance. Missional leaders know that praise should be done publicly, but criticism of individuals should be done privately. I have been called upon many times over the years to speak a word of private criticism to people in the church as well as to the church staff. I have learned it is extremely important that this communication be done in a particular way. The clear teaching of Scripture is needed here. The Apostle Paul shares the God-intended results of spiritual maturity. A part of full spiritual development for missional leaders is learning about *"speaking the truth in love"* (Ephesians 4:15).

It is important we speak the truth if we want to grow, and if we want others to grow in every way into Christ. Communication must occur on both corporate and individual levels, with a balance of praise and criticism. Either way, we must speak the truth. If there was ever a time the world needed objective truth, it is now. Our society has swallowed Satan's lies and gone totally off balance, skewed in every respect, being led down a slippery slope toward moral anarchy and abandonment of common sense.

"But speaking the truth in love, let us grow in every way into Him who is the head—Christ." There are different ways Ephesians 4:15 can be translated. Some translate it, *"dealing truly in love,"* or *"hold by the truth,"* or *"speaking truth in love."* The problem is that there is no verb for *truth* in English, while there is in Greek. What Paul is actually saying is, "truthing in love." The basic concept is that our manner of life is to be sincere and true, thinking truly, speaking truly, dealing truly, and all of this in a spirit of genuine love, without diversions to divide our allegiance, without hypocrisy to deny our witness, and without divisions to hinder our purpose in Him. Truthing in love is what we are called to do.

In Matthew 7, Jesus speaks about being on guard against false prophets (15–16). Why would Jesus say to beware of false prophets if there were no false prophets or false teachings? The obvious answer is that this word of warning was and is applicable, because the enemy is a liar and the father of lies (John 8:44).

Through the centuries, the devil has spun his dangerously and intricately woven web of deceit through all human enterprises, including religion, philosophy, emotions, and relationships. While many in the world are speaking falsely, it is obligatory for the missional leader to speak truthfully in love.

Do we as missional leaders back away from saying certain things because we know it will hurt feelings? Do we tailor our messages to get the loudest "amens," knowing we are hitting on subjects favored by the audience? Do we ignore certain issues and certain sins, because we are afraid to offend someone and we might possibly lose our job? Yet, God calls us to speak the truth and to do it in season and out of season. We need more prophets in leadership willing to be bold enough to do what God says.

But we must speak the truth in love. Our world has written us off, marginalized us as being incapable of serious thought. The most damning criticism the world has leveled against us is not that we are incapable of serious thought, however, but that we are devoid of love. The caricature of the Bible-pounding, Scripture-quoting, hateful, screaming preacher has become a part of the American conception of religion. This world will not be won by harsh tirades, but by missional leaders speaking the truth clearly, but in love, so that the love and passion of Christ comes through. This is *agape* love, God's kind of love, without end, limit, or condition.

The early church was met with much horrific persecution. They were also met with acceptance by those who chose the narrow way. The distinction between the two couldn't have been clearer. But today, in a world that considers Christianity mostly irrelevant, the vast majority of people respond with a yawn. We need to speak the truth in love! We need to *"walk in wisdom toward outsiders, making the most of the time. Your speech should always be gracious, seasoned with salt, so that we may know how to answer each person"* (Colossians 4:5–6).

I have already said this, but it bears repeating: Truth without love leads to a coldhearted legalism, and love without truth leads to a liberalism leaving people bereft of direction.

Missional leaders are desperately needed to show our world we are more than unsophisticated rustics without the capacity for intelligence and without modern cultural relevance. We do have a message, the greatest message of them all, and it needs to be communicated clearly: God does care and can make a difference in our lives.

In my own setting, I have tried to communicate, as best I can, by speaking the truth in love. Sometimes communication must be very creative, sometimes even humorous, when one is speaking truthfully as well as lovingly. The US standard railroad gauge (distance between rails) is four feet, eight-and-one-half inches. Why such an odd number? Because that's the way they built them in England, and US railroads were built by the British expatriates. Why did the English themselves adopt that particular gauge as standard? Because the people who built the prerailroad tramways used that gauge. They in turn were locked into that gauge because the people who built tramways used the same standards and tools they had used for building wagons that were set on a gauge of four feet, eight-and-one-half inches. Why were wagons built to that scale? Because with any other size, the wheels did not match the old wheel ruts on the roads. Who built these old rutted roads? The first long-distance highways in Europe were built by Imperial Rome for the benefit of their legions. The roads have been in use ever since. The ruts were first made by Roman war chariots. Four feet, eight-and-one-half inches was the width a chariot needed to be to accommodate the rear ends of two war horses.

We love our traditions very much, and change is not easy. Many people in churches want change to occur, so long as the pastor does not change the things they really like! To communicate the need for change requires patience, love, and the ability to lovingly, truthfully share the reality of what is happening.

The church I am privileged to pastor has a long and interesting history. Founded in 1864, it followed the way of many churches in growth and decline. Following the economics of the area, it had both periods of glory and periods of despair. Even though the area has been growing mightily for the last 20 years, the church began to plateau in 1993 and then began to decline in 1997. I am thankful the Lord has shown new life to our old church. We are now almost three times the size we were in 2001. Our baptisms have risen to the highest level in the history of the congregation. God has been infusing life back into our fellowship. This change did not come easily and it did not come quickly. It came through much patience, prayer, love, and the art of communicating truth in love. It is the scriptural methodology missional leaders must master.

Reflections

1. How and why was Nehemiah a missional leader of communication?

2. What does Paul really mean when he says *"speaking the truth in love"*?

3. Explain: "Truth without love leads to a coldhearted legalism, and love without truth leads to a liberalism leaving people bereft of direction."

CHAPTER 14

A Missional Leader
Is a Great Time Manager

Missional leaders know the need for effective time management. I believe a missional leader has to be an effective time manager. We must learn how to balance life in such a way as to manage time appropriately. I have known many preachers who have delivered sermons on the priorities of time, resources, and life management. They often give a list: God is number one, family is number two, church is number three, and work is number four. But the truth is that people who try living with that priority list in mind find themselves deeply discouraged much of the time. Artificial lists will always lead to that kind of discouragement.

The Bible tells us to *"seek first the kingdom of God and His righteousness, and all these things will be provided for you"* (Matthew 6:33). I believe God's people should seek a kingdom priority. In other words, if we seek the kingdom of God and His righteousness as the number one priority of our lives, He will so order our lives that we will have all aspects in harmony and balance. Nothing will be out of kilter.

Nehemiah had this kind of balance in life. He wrote, *"When I heard these words I sat down and wept. I mourned for a number of days, fasting and praying before the God of heaven"* (1:4). With his focus totally on the Lord, Nehemiah spent days fasting and praying before God. During those days, his focus was not on work, or family, or anything else other than the heavenly Father. I believe Nehemiah was not a man to neglect family or work, and we must never neglect them, either. But when God directs our lives, we will be in total balance.

Nehemiah had a strong practice of delegation. In the third chapter, we see the delegation to a variety of groups of specific tasks relating to the rebuilding of the walls. He was well aware the work was far too much for him to do alone. He used the skills and gifts of the people as appropriate. An example of his delegation practice is when Nehemiah said, *"I put my brother Hanani in charge of Jerusalem, along with Hananiah, commander of the fortress, because he was a faithful man who feared God more than most"* (7:2). The women were also a part of the effort. *"Beside him Shallum son of Hallohesh, ruler over half the district of Jerusalem, made repairs—he and his daughters"* (3:12).

> **When God directs our lives, we will be in total balance.**

I imagine the greatest example of time management is that of our Lord Jesus. He never seemed to be overly busy. For many people in our world today, being called "busy" is a compliment. But it should not be so. To be busy means we are probably doing too much. Christ was never too busy to stop and speak with a woman, a child, a poor person, or any person in need. He had perfect balance in His life. Though the multitudes followed Him and attempted to spend time with Him, Jesus seems to have had the perfect balance to know when to spend time with them and when to get away on his own. *"Jesus departed with His disciples to the sea, and a great multitude followed from Galilee, Judea, Jerusalem, Idumea, beyond the Jordan, and around Tyre and Sidon."* (Mark 3:7–8). The public came to Him because they heard about everything he was doing. Yet, *"very early in the morning, while it was still dark, He got up, went out, and made His way to a deserted place. And He was praying there"* (Mark 1:35). Jesus knew when He needed to have time to be alone, when He needed to spend serious teaching time with His disciples, and when He needed to spend time with the crowds. He must have been a master at time management.

In the book *Freedom from Busyness*, Michael Zigarelli shares the results of a large survey he conducted.

- To the statement: "The busyness of my life gets in the way of developing my relationship with God," six out of ten (60 percent) responded that this is often or always true of them.
- To the statement: "I rush from task to task," more than four out of ten (43 percent) said this is often or always true of them.
- About half (49 percent) said they often or always eat quickly, and about one in three (30 percent) admitted they often or always hurry even when I don't have to.
- "It appears that many Christians are doing way too many things at a pace that's way too fast. As a result, we're distracted from God and we're overloaded, even exhausted. In fact, one out of two Christians (51%) in my survey said that they're often or always 'exhausted at the end of my day,' and another 24% said this is true of them sometimes. That's a lot of tired Christians."

Would you not agree that most of us are simply too busy? Our hectic activity is not only causing us to be too busy for attention to God, too busy for our husbands, wives, and children, but also too busy for friendships—and certainly too busy for rest.

Perhaps one of the greatest lessons in busyness and priority is found when the Lord answered Martha. *"Martha, Martha, you are worried and upset about many things, but one thing is necessary. Mary has made the right choice, and it will not be taken away from her"* (Luke 10:41–42). The admonishing words of our Lord Jesus to Martha indicate the need to make the "right choice" when it comes to the way we spend our time. Many time managers teach how to crowd more activity and work into the same period of time. I am convinced that the better approach is learning how to make the right choice. We must learn to become very open to the Holy Spirit, who no doubt wishes us free from the tyranny of the urgent. It is all right to say no to some things. God will lead us to say yes to the right things.

> God will lead us to say yes to the right things.

One of the issues troubling Christians is the urge toward perfectionism. Paul writes, *"For am I now trying to win the favor of people, or God? Or am I striving to please people? If I were still trying to please people, I would not be a slave of Christ"* (Galatians 1:10). In our society, we are pushed to please other people and be perfect in everything we do. Many people I know define themselves by what they do, so they want to be the best at what they do to feel good about themselves. But the value of a person does not depend on what we do or what others think of us.

The Scriptures indicate that our value has nothing to do with accomplishments or our perfection in human activities. God only wants us to please Him.

Think back. What are the best times you remember as a child? Wouldn't it be the times of greatest blessings were those occasions spent meaningfully with your family? In a spiritual sense, I can assure you the greatest blessings come from the time spent with the Lord. Let us remember who to please and how to please.

Missional leaders need to become people who know how to say yes and no at the appropriate times. There needs to be the ability to work smart, not just hard. The missional leader needs to learn how to "multitask" and use electronic technology to his or her own benefit. I remind you that our ultimate example is that of our Lord Jesus Christ. His freedom from busyness enabled Him to be the true missional leader to those who followed Him.

Reflections

1. What is the key to managing time appropriately?

2. Given the Lord's answer to Martha to stop worrying about things, what lesson on busyness and priority are we to learn?

3. How can we free ourselves from busyness?

CHAPTER 15

A Missional Leader
Is Willing to Provide Accountability

Day 1: I walk down the street; there is a deep hole in the sidewalk. I fall in, I am lost, I am helpless. It isn't my fault. It takes forever to find a way out.

Day 2: I walk down the street; there is a deep hole in the sidewalk. I pretend I don't see it, I fall in. I can't believe I am in the same place, but it isn't my fault. It still takes me a long time to get out.

Day 3: I walk down the street; there is a deep hole in the sidewalk. I see it there...I still fall in. It is a habit, my eyes are open, I know where I am. It is my fault.

Day 4: I walk down the street; there is a deep hole in the sidewalk. I walk around it.

Day 5: I walk down a different street.

A Divine Audit

This story speaks about the power of habit. It speaks about a growing realization of the need to make a decisive move to end or break a bad habit. Wouldn't it be good if we could all break our bad habits? Wouldn't it be great if we could be freed from evil strongholds, bad tendencies, and all the egregious sins in our lives?

Our church does a financial audit every year. Like most churches, this is an important part of making sure that finances are correctly administered. It is always an important part of our financial management. As usual, our church was blessed to have a wonderful report from our most recent audit. If there was a divine auditor who could give us a multipage questionnaire detailing and evaluating each part of our lives, what would such an audit show? Each of us, in our honest moments, knows that the Holy Spirit of God is the divine auditor. He is the revealer of thoughts, the judge of actions and behavior. What does the Lord reveal about our lives? Does He betray that we are progressing in our growth in Him? Does He show we are willing to be accountable not only to His still small voice, but to the accountability of others as well?

There is an interesting place in Scripture where the people of God were held accountable, not to one of God's prophets, but actually to an angel. The story is in the Book of Judges.

And an angel of the LORD came up from Gilgal to Bochim, and said, I made you to go up out of Egypt, and have brought you unto the land which I sware unto your fathers; and I said, I will never break my covenant with you. And ye shall make no league with the inhabitants of this land; ye shall throw down their altars: but ye have not obeyed my voice: why have ye done this? Wherefore I also said, I will not drive them out from before you; but they shall be as thorns in your sides, and their gods shall be a snare unto you. And it came to pass, when the angel of the LORD spake these words unto all the children of Israel, that the people lifted up their voice, and wept. And they called the name of that place Bochim: and they

sacrificed there unto the LORD. And when Joshua had let the people go, the children of Israel went every man unto his inheritance to possess the land. And the people served the LORD all the days of Joshua, and all the days of the elders that outlived Joshua, who had seen all the great works of the LORD, that he did for Israel.
—Judges 2:1–7 (KJV)

In this passage, God sent His angel to preach. This angel was of one essence with the Father and spoke directly with the Father's message. The angel's words were quite direct: *"I made you to go up out of Egypt, and have brought you unto the land;...I said, I will never break my covenant with you....But ye have not obeyed my voice: why have ye done this?"* (KJV)

God blessed them, but the people broke their agreement with God. They failed. They intermarried with the heathen Canaanites and adopted their foreign practice of idol worship. They disobeyed God in not destroying the evil altars of the Canaanites, and they embraced the ways of the heathen religions. The angel's question, *"Why have ye done this?"* (KJV) brought guilt and grief. This question could be asked of us too. "Why have you done this?" Judges says that *"the people lifted up their voice, and wept."* (KJV) These tears were tears of regret. When God's angel confronted them, a great outpouring came forth. The conviction of the people's sins brought sorrow. They could have denied the angel's claim, as we often do. But they were convicted.

We put on a front in claiming to be obedient. We have become great experts at living untrue lives. We have become quite proficient in putting on superspiritual fronts. I heard recently of a story of a four-year-old-boy who was asked to return thanks before Christmas dinner. The family members bowed their heads in expectation. He began his prayer, thanking

God for all his friends, naming them one by one. Then he thanked God for Mommy, Daddy, Brother, Sister, Grandma, Grandpa, and all his aunts and uncles. Then he began to thank God for the food. He gave thanks for the turkey, the dressing, the fruit salad, the cranberry sauce, the pies, the cakes, even the whipped topping. Then he paused, and everyone waited—and waited. After a long silence, the young fellow looked up at his mother and asked, "If I thank God for the broccoli, won't He know that I'm lying?" We need to learn the lesson of honesty that little boy teaches, instead of putting on a false facade.

God's people could have gotten angry and gotten their feelings hurt, as we often do. Instead, they wept tears of regret. Even the place where the experience happened was forever called *Bokim*, which means "a weeping place."

The end result of dishonesty and disobedience is hurt and sorrow, not a life of happiness and pleasure. It is pain. Instead of having the best of two worlds, the Hebrews found that disobeying God through idol worship became a snare to them. Perhaps even worse was the fact that their disobedience led their children to even worse pain. *"That whole generation was also gathered to their ancestors. After them another generation rose up who did not know the Lord or the works He had done for Israel"* (2:10).

> If you let God take second place, then you have given Him last place.

In the story of Dr. Jekyll and Mr. Hyde, Dr. Jekyll was a gentleman, a scientist who developed a potion that transformed him into an evil, cruel being. After using this potion several times, the evil became so dominant that he permanently became Mr. Hyde. The point I want to make of this is if you give sin an inch, it will take a mile. If you let God take second place, then you have given Him last place. You will lead yourself to sorrow, to pain, to tears of regret. You will end up asking, "Why have I done this?"

At times we need pain and the shedding of tears of regret. The tears must have a stopping point, however. If not, the regret can paralyze us. David Lloyd George, prime minister of Great Britain during World War I, was taking a walk with a friend one day. Each time they walked through a gate, George would close it after them. The friend saw what he was doing. "You don't need to close those gates," the friend said. "The caretakers will do that."

"Yes, I think I do," replied George. "You see, I've spent my life shutting gates behind me. A wise person always does that. When one shuts a gate behind himself, the past is held there."

Shedding tears of regret is like closing the gates behind us. We can't change or erase our past sins, but we can shut the gate on them. Let us shed tears of regret, and then close the gate. In the Judges text, the tears were tears of repentance. Scripture says the people *"sacrificed there unto the LORD"* (KJV). They were most likely presenting sin offerings and burnt offerings, that they might obtain mercy and forgiveness. In any event, they repented and turned to the living God. Deeply regretting their actions, they decided to do something about it. Instead of lamenting their plight, they repented and sacrificed to the Lord. God's continuing love for His people in the midst of their sins is a beautiful picture of the Father's grace. We have violated His covenant and we deserve no mercy. We are sinners in need of redemption. Repentance is the first step on the road of spiritual recovery.

Mind-Altering Repentance

Repentance implies much more than a "change of mind." It is actually a changing of the *state* of one's mind. It is a conversion, a reorientation of the personality. Jesus said, *"Those who are well don't need a doctor, but the sick do need one. I didn't come to call the righteous, but sinners"* (Mark 2:17). We need to shed tears of regret and real, true repentance. It is a sad thing to say, but I believe many who today have their names on the rolls of the church will never see their names placed on the roll of heaven, because they've never genuinely repented. They have not let go of anything, and they think they can hold on to all of the flesh and at the same moment be possessed of the Spirit of God. Tears of repentance are required.

I heard of a 14-year-old girl, who had only recently become a Christian, offering a brilliant definition of *repentance*. Aware that the girl was unusual and also that she came from a home where she had little encouragement, the Sunday School teacher wanted to help her all she could. One Sunday the lesson was on repentance, and the teacher said to the young girl, "Margaret, do you think you could explain to the class what *repentance* means?"

Margaret shyly faced the class, and, in a clear voice, said, "I think it means this: Before I was saved, I pleased myself, and wasn't a bit sorry for my sins. In fact, I didn't think I was a sinner at all; but when I accepted Christ, I wanted to please Him above everyone, and was sorry I ever grieved Him. I love to please Him now."

You won't find a better definition of *repentance* than that.

The end result was that *"the people served the LORD all the days of Joshua"* (KJV). After the Israelites learned to regret their ways, and after they repented, they were able to rejoice. They were able to see clearly what God had done for them. The great works of the Lord are cause for rejoicing in any generation. Fulfillment took the place of emptiness, and service took the place of sorrow. Life had meaning.

> **Missional leaders must hold their people responsible and provide accountability.**

The same experience was a part of the lives of many people found in Scripture. Simon Peter experienced the tears of failure and he also experienced repentance and rejoicing in the Lord's forgiveness, as he was held accountable by the Lord. The prodigal son experienced his *Bokim,* or weeping place, in a pigpen. His experience of guilt and tears brought tender repentance and overwhelming rejoicing. And there are many, many others.

Wouldn't it be wonderful to be held accountable by the presence of an angel? Indeed, we, too, would cry tears of regret and repentance, but in the final analysis we would be restored and we would be rejoicing. I believe that missional leaders must hold their people responsible and provide accountability so that they, too, can experience the results that God's people experienced in the Book of Judges.

Nehemiah was a missional leader who believed in accountability. For example, we know that he held others accountable. In fact, Nehemiah's witness for the Lord was exemplified in the manner in which he corrected those who transgressed the law or failed in their duties. In 13:17, Nehemiah rebuked the officials regarding their neglect of important responsibilities, including the Sabbath day. *"I rebuked the nobles of Judah and said to them: 'What is this evil you are doing— profaning the Sabbath day?'"* He also rebuked the officials in 13:11: *"Therefore, I rebuked the officials, saying, 'Why has the house of God been neglected?' I gathered the Levites and singers together and stationed them at their posts."*

And Nehemiah wrote,

> *Then I instructed the Levites to purify themselves and guard the gates in order to keep the Sabbath day holy. Remember me for this also, my God, and look on me with compassion in keeping with Your abundant, faithful love.*
> —Nehemiah 13:22

He also called the people to accountability. He said,

> *I rebuked them, cursed them, beat some of their men, and pulled out their hair. I forced them to take an oath before God and said: "You must not give your daughters in marriage to their sons or take their daughters as wives for your sons or yourselves!"*
> —Nehemiah 13:25

Today it would be a rarity to see someone who literally pulls the hair out of those over whom they are given authority. How times have changed!

Nehemiah was not only one who believed in the accountability of others, he was willing to hold himself up to the same standards of accountability.

> *Furthermore, from the day King Artaxerxes appointed me to be their governor in the land of Judah—from the twentieth year until his thirty-second year, 12 years— I and my associates never ate from the food allotted to the governor.*
> —Nehemiah 5:14

Nehemiah's sensitivity as well as accountability was also evident where he said, *"I didn't demand the food allotted to the governor, because the burden on the people was so heavy"* (5:18).

Nehemiah's accountability and submission to the king is powerfully obvious when he said, *"If it pleases the king, and if your servant has found favor with you, send me to Judah and to the city where my ancestors are buried, so that I may rebuild it"* (2:5). Nehemiah was a missional leader who believed in accountability.

> He was willing to hold himself up to the same standards of accountability.

Every true missional leader needs to submit himself or herself to accountability. It may be through some kind of official church board or it may be through an informal group of friends. But every person needs to be accountable to at least one person who will ask the right questions at the right time. I've often said that every person needs a Paul, a Timothy, and a Barnabas.

Everybody needs someone to look up to such as a Paul who can mentor and guide. This is more important during the earlier times of spiritual growth, obviously, but every person needs to be mentoring or helping someone else. As we grow and mature in the Lord, this becomes an extremely important part of our personal ministry. Everyone needs to take alongside themselves a young Timothy type to help him or her. No one should be without a Barnabas, an encourager, a friend. We need to place ourselves in accountability with someone who loves us enough to be unconditional in their love, and sometimes even pointed in their questioning.

Reflections

1. How did the Israelites break their agreement with God?

2. How would you answer the angel's question, *"Why have ye done this?"*

3. How is shedding tears of regret like closing the door behind us? What does real repentance imply?

CHAPTER 16

A Missional Leader
Is a Person Who Celebrates Victory

Many people in life are very negative, and we have all met some of them. As you read these actual newspaper ads, think of the negative people you have known:

FREE Yorkshire Terrier. 8 years old. Hateful little dog. Bites.
FREE Puppies. ½ Cocker Spaniel, ½ sneaky neighbor's dog.
FREE Puppies. Part German Shepherd, part stupid dog.
FREE German Shepherd. 85 lbs. Neutered. Speaks German.
Found Dirty White Dog. Looks like a rat...been out a while...better be a reward.
Nordic Track. $300 hardly used, call Chubby.
Georgia Peaches. California. 89 cents/lb.
Wedding Dress for Sale. Worn once by mistake. Call Stephanie.

Despite the fact that there is much negativity in this world, there are also many positive things to celebrate. In fact, the missional leader is a person who knows how to celebrate victory. Nehemiah was that kind of missional leader. He said, *"When the wall had been rebuilt and I had the doors installed, the gatekeepers, singers, and Levites were appointed"* (7:1). It was a day for celebration.

> *Nehemiah the governor, Ezra the priest and scribe, and the Levites who were instructing the people said to all of them, "This day is holy to the LORD your God. Do not mourn or weep." For all the people were weeping as they heard the words of the law.*
> —Nehemiah 8:9

And the next verse says, *"Do not grieve, because your strength comes from rejoicing in the LORD."* It truly was a day of rejoicing and celebration. God had blessed and now it was time to celebrate. The missional leader encourages God's people to a celebration of the goodness of God.

The parable that best shows the goodness of God is often called the parable of the prodigal son. But actually, Luke 15:11–32 tells the story of two prodigals. The well-known son who went to the far country was certainly a prodigal. The older brother who stayed at home, however, was a prodigal in his heart. The true hero of the story is the loving father. That is why I prefer to call this the parable of the loving father. The point connecting the teaching of this story with a missional leader's life has to do with the party given when the younger son returned home. *"Then bring the fattened calf and slaughter it, and let's celebrate with a feast, because this son of mine was dead and is alive again; he was lost and is found! So they began to celebrate"* (15:23–24). This was not a fellowship—it was a party! The family had a

> **The missional leader encourages God's people to a celebration of the goodness of God.**

great party that day to celebrate the homecoming, the spiritual victory that occurred in the young son's life. Missional leaders should lead God's people in celebrating how good our God is.

Seizing the Season

King David was one who knew how to celebrate victory. In 1 Chronicles the chronicler says, *"Michal looked down from the window and saw King David dancing and celebrating."* (15:29). Missional leaders know how to celebrate victory. They know people need encouragement. They know people eager for the kingdom have expended a great amount of energy and need a time of relaxation and rejoicing over spiritual victories. In the midst of a very negative world, missional leaders know how to set aside a time to give their people that time, that season of celebration.

I have often felt that one of the results of providing leadership in my local setting is the dramatic change in perspective and expectancy in our church fellowship. Many congregants, some of whom have been in the church for years, state there is a new life and joy in our worship services. Those are words every pastor loves to hear. Perhaps we have made some strides toward realizing that the way of Christ is the way of joy, peace, and inner contentment. This reality is powerfully expressed in what I have often called my favorite verse in all the Bible, John 10:10, *"A thief comes only to steal and to kill and to destroy. I have come that they may have life and have it in abundance."* To me, that is the quintessential description of spiritual warfare, good versus evil, the greatest expression of theology, and a great encouragement in missions and evangelism. This verse reveals the work of the archenemy, the Evil One, in a succinct yet powerful fashion. Note that Jesus uses the word *only*, and this means Satan's work will always lead to hurt and destruction. Despite the fact that he has a way of disguising himself and his desires with beautiful appointments, the ultimate result is always disaster. Jesus calls him the thief. He comes only to steal and destroy.

What has the thief stolen from you? Has he already been able to steal your dreams, your visions, and your hopes for the future? Has he pilfered your testimony of purity and power? What has he done to the churches? He has stolen effectiveness, power, and the sweet attractiveness that draws the lost into the kingdom of God? What has he stolen from our Convention? Exactly the same...our power, our effectiveness, our unity, and the sweet testimony which draws the world to Christ. The thief has done his work effectively.

Jesus says the thief has also come to kill and to destroy. Normally, we do not think of a thief as one who comes to kill or destroy. But think about it at a deeper level. The thief destroys many things, including one's security. Reflect on what Satan has killed in your life, in the lives of family and friends, in our churches, and in our denominations. He is the absolute master at killing personal dreams. He is the consummate authority when it comes to destroying unity in churches and creating factions even within our own Convention. Didn't Jesus Himself say,

> *"I pray not only for these, but also for those who believe in Me through their message. May they all be one, as You, Father, are in Me and I am in You. May they also be one in Us, so the world may believe You sent Me."*
> —John 17:20–21

What happened to that prayer request of Jesus's? Satan, with our acquiescence, has destroyed hope, unity, and integrity of Christians in many, if not most, situations.

As president of the Southern Baptist Convention, news media, both religious and secular, constantly sought my opinion.

One of the things I have said to them is simply that for a long time Baptists have been known for what we are *against*, not what we are *for*. There is a legitimate reason for this, because sometimes we have had to take stands against things in our society that are clearly wrong. We will continue to do so. And at times it is because the media, having to make choices about what they report, choose the most salacious, embarrassing, and sometimes the most egregious of acts or comments on which to report. Better for the ratings. I have asked them at each interview, to give us a chance to tell the world what we are for. Give us a chance to say we believe in a personal relationship with a Lord Jesus that can change lives and transform families. Let us tell you what we are for, not what we are against. Maybe if we tell people what we are for rather than always what we are against, the prayer request of Jesus will be thwarted no more. The Evil One is so good at what he does bad.

"A thief comes only to steal and to kill and to destroy. I have come that they may have life and have it in abundance." Here we also see the work of the Savior. Jesus tells of His ultimate purpose, which is the antithesis to Satan's purpose. Jesus says He comes to give us life that is abundant, full, and transcendent.

What does the Lord mean by *life*? He defines this in many places and in many ways. John 3:16 tells of the eternal life we have when we personally receive Him into our hearts and minds as Lord and Savior. *"For God loved the world in this way: He gave his One and Only Son, so that everyone who believes in Him will not perish but have eternal life."* He describes this eternal life in John 17:3 as knowing the only true God, and Jesus Christ. Eternal life to Jesus is not a matter of a calendar but a relationship.

If there was ever a day when Christ's followers required new life in our denominations, churches, parachurch organizations, families, and personal lives, it's now. Thank God that He brings life to all who would follow Him. It's time to celebrate that life.

A sailing vessel ran out of fresh water as it traveled across the South Atlantic Ocean. The crew was thirsty to the point of despair. But help appeared when they sighted another vessel. As the vessels approached one another, the sailors from the drought-ridden ship called for help to those on the other ship. "Please give us water to drink; we have no water and we are almost to die" was their plea. A strange reply came from the other ship, "Let down your buckets where you are." The request went back again for fresh water. The same response came from the other ship, "Let down your buckets where you are." Finally, in desperation, the sailors dying of thirst lowered their buckets down into the water and found the water they pulled back up was fresh water, not salt water. They did not realize they had arrived near the mouth of the mighty Amazon River. The force and volume of the water out of the Amazon is so powerful that the water actually stays fresh for many, many miles out into the salty ocean. The ship was actually floating in fresh water and the men did not know it. The sailors were saved.

> Thank God that He brings life. It is now time to celebrate that life.

I think the Lord is telling us it is time to let down our buckets. The only way we are going to live life abundantly is to let our buckets down into the available life-giving ministry of the Holy Spirit of God. Let us celebrate the fact that God makes this available to us! Let us rejoice in the power He has given for us to become missional leaders!

Reflections

1. How can missional leaders best encourage Christians to a celebration of the goodness of God?

2. How is the thief able to steal one's dreams, visions, and hopes?

3. What does the Lord mean by *life*?

Conclusion

At the dedication of the wall of Jerusalem, they sent for the Levites wherever they lived and brought them to Jerusalem to celebrate the joyous dedication with thanksgiving and singing accompanied by symbols, harps, and lyres.
—Nehemiah 12:27

God had done a great work among His people. The leadership—the *missional* leadership of Nehemiah—had brought effectiveness and victory to the task. A vision that had begun during a time of prayer and fasting had now come to fruition. Thousands of hours of work, opposition by the enemy, and difficulties of various kinds presented themselves along the way. However, the factors present in the missional leadership of Nehemiah were used by God to overcome all obstacles and see the accomplishment of God's will.

The last phrase in the Book of Nehemiah is as follows, *"Remember me, my God, with favor"* (13:31). What a way to end a Bible book! Wouldn't it be great if that last phrase were the last words coming forth from our lips before we meet the Lord in eternity? Even the last words of the book indicate humility and a prayerful spirit. Nehemiah was a great example of a missional leader.

How can we end our lives with that same kind of leadership? This passage tells us.

> *Now may the God of peace, who brought up from the dead our Lord Jesus—the great Shepherd of the sheep—with the blood of the everlasting covenant, equip you with all that is good to do His will, working in us what is pleasing in His sight, through Jesus Christ, to whom be glory forever and ever. Amen.*
> —Hebrews 13:20–21

Missional leaders, take heed!

Bibliography

Blackaby, Henry, and Richard Blackaby. *Spiritual Leadership*. Nashville: Broadman & Holman Publishers, 2001.

Fant, Clyde. *Preaching for Today*. New York: Harper & Row, Publishers, 1975.

Farrar, Steve. *Point Man*. Portland: Multnomah Press, 1990.

Graham, Billy. *Just As I Am*. New York: HarperCollins Publishers, 1997.

Kramp, John. *On Track Leadership*. Nashville: Broadman & Holman Publishers, 2006.

Martin, William. *A Prophet with Honor*. New York: William Morrow & Company, 1991.

Reed, Eric, and Collin Hansen. "How Pastors Rate as Leaders: Leadership Surveys Pastors and Their Congregations." *Leadership Journal* (Fall 2003): 30.

Smith, David W. *The Friendless American Male*. Ventura, CA: Regal Books, 1983.

Zigarelli, Michael. *Freedom from Busyness*. Nashville: LifeWay Press, 2005.

New Hope® Publishers is a division of WMU®, an international organization that challenges Christian believers to understand and be radically involved in God's mission. For more information about WMU, go to www.wmu.com. More information about New Hope books may be found at www.newhopepublishers.com. New Hope books may be purchased at your local bookstore.

More Books on
Leadership

Good for Goodness' Sake
7 Values for Cultivating
Authentic Character in Midlife
Gary Fenton
ISBN-10: 1-59669-009-7
ISBN-13: 978-1-59669-009-7

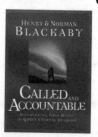

Called and Accountable
Discovering Your Place
in God's Eternal Purpose
Henry T. Blackaby and Norman C. Blackaby
(trade book)
ISBN-10: 1-59669-047-X
ISBN-13: 978-1-59669-047-9

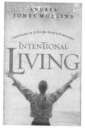

Intentional Living
Choosing to Live
for God's Purposes
Andrea Jones Mullins
ISBN-10: 1-56309-927-6
ISBN-13: 978-1-56309-927-4

TeamsWork
A No-Nonsense Approach
for Achieving More Together
Joyce A. Mitchell
ISBN-10: 1-59669-211-1
ISBN-13: 978-1-59669-211-4

Available in bookstores everywhere

For information about these books or any New Hope product,
visit www.newhopepublishers.com.